If You Don't Know Me, Don't Judge Me

www.transworldireland.ie

www.rbooks.co.uk

If You Don't Know Me, Don't Judge Me

My Autobiography

Dan Shanahan

TRANSWORLD IRELAND

TRANSWORLD IRELAND
an imprint of The Random House Group Limited
20 Vauxhall Bridge Road, London SW1V 2SA
www.rbooks.co.uk

First published in 2010 by Transworld Ireland,
a division of Transworld Publishers

A CIP catalogue record for this book
is available from the British Library.

ISBN 9781848270985

Addresses for Random House Group Ltd companies outside the UK
can be found at: www.randomhouse.co.uk
The Random House Group Ltd Reg. No. 954009

The Random House Group Limited supports the Forest Stewardship
Council (FSC), the leading international forest-certification organization. All our
titles that are printed on Greenpeace-approved FSC-certified paper carry the FSC
logo. Our paper procurement policy can be found at
www.rbooks.co.uk/environment

Typeset in 11.5/16pt Berling by
Falcon Oast Graphic Art Ltd.
Printed and bound in Great Britain by
Clays Ltd, Bungay, Suffolk

4 6 8 10 9 7 5 3

I would like to dedicate this book to
my parents, Mary and Brian Shanahan,
and my late grandmother, Mary Jo Shanahan.

Acknowledgements

If you read this book you'll understand how much my family means to me; I want to thank my mother and father, Mary and Brian, my sisters Pauline and Sharon, and my brothers James and Maurice.

My extended family deserve thanks as well – Donal, Ann and family; Tom, Nora and family; Joan, Dando and family; Breda, Kathleen, Mikey and family; Noreen, Michael and family; Eileen, Tom and family; Margaret, my nan Mary, and my late grandmother Mary Jo; also, Maurice and Bernie, Marie, Valerie, Helen, Nicola, Antoinette, Edel and especially Shelly and Emma, as well as Trevor and Maurice Whelan.

To all the people I have worked with in Cappoquin Bacon Factory and Waterford Crystal (Dungarvan plant) – thank you.

To my colleagues in East Cork Oil, especially Des Hurley – thanks a million for your support. To Paddy Joe Ryan, Caroline, John, Michael, David, Nicky, Maurice, Cathal, Catherine and all the customers – thanks for all your support over the years.

A special thanks to my primary and secondary school teachers, and to all my team-mates, including those that I didn't mention in this book by name.

I would like to thank Helena and Donnacha Gough of the Local Bar; and Mary and Billy Foley of Paddy Foley's Bar; and Eamonn Walsh of Eamonn's Place, Lismore, not forgetting the rest of the staff and customers of these establishments for all your support over the years.

Soldiering with Waterford for fourteen years meant togging off with some great men: it was a privilege. It was also a privilege to play for the supporters, who stood by us through thick and thin. I would also like to thank the backroom team, hurley carriers and especially Jim Dee, Roger Casey and Tommy Burns. My thanks also go to all the trainers with Lismore GAA and Waterford GAA and to Ross Barrett (Cappoquin MMA).

Thanks to Michael Moynihan, Martin Doyle (Opel), Paul Moloney (Adidas), Noel Devereux, Sean Power from Harvey Travel, Tom Murphy and Ger Wyley Sports. To Glanbia and Kieran O'Connor – thanks a lot. And my special thanks to Dr Mark Rowe, Ray Kelly and Dr Tom Higgins.

To the patriots of Lismore, especially the residents of Parks Road – thank you so much – your support has been fantastic and greatly appreciated. To Lismore GAA – it has been a pleasure to know you and to play with you – I would not be where I am only for you.

To all my friends who have been there with me in good times and bad: you know who you are. Thank you so much – especially Chicken.

To all those who have now passed on in Lismore GAA and Waterford GAA – *Ar dheis Dé go raibh a n-anamacha.*

A very special thank you to Eddie O'Donnell for everything he has done for me over the years.

Last but not least, Colette and Chloe – don't think I don't appreciate the sacrifices you've made for me. After fourteen years I'm looking forward to that holiday.

As it is impossible to thank everyone, and for those of you I may have omitted to mention – a big thank you.

Prologue

The day was wrong from the start.

We had players injured, players dropped and players cranky. Not what you need going out to play Clare in the first round of the Munster senior hurling championship in 2008.

When we got to Limerick there was another cock-up. After a bite to eat we were out in the blazing sun before the game, hitting a few balls around in grass up to our shins, nearly losing the *sliotar* in the undergrowth. We'd always gone to a club pitch for a puck-around, yet here we were in a hayfield instead, the grass up over our ankles, pucking around before heading to the Gaelic Grounds.

Then the Garda escort broke down on the way to the game. While we sat roasting on the bus the manager, Justin McCarthy, got out a CD of music he wanted to us to listen to, presumably to get us geed up for the game. Too little, too late. It was all wrong.

In the game John Mullane played well, Tony Browne, Dave Bennett and Michael 'Brick' Walsh were very good, but Clare won well. I was beaten off the field by Conor Plunkett (who I hurled in 2004), one of those days when wherever you go the ball falls behind you or in front of you, but never comes to you handy.

I was injured and I shouldn't have played, but I lined out. Plunkett must have had a pain in his back from leathering the ball up the field. I couldn't get involved in the game and seemed to spend the entire time arriving just as Plunkett blasted another clearance ninety yards down the field. In the end, I wasn't surprised to see my number being held up – I was to be taken off.

I was annoyed with myself, and injured, and obviously I didn't enjoy getting the call from the sideline, but as I came off the field I made the biggest mistake of my life. Justin stuck his hand out to shake, the normal procedure from the manager when you're getting hauled ashore, and I didn't take it. I just brushed past him.

There was a roar from the crowd – the match wasn't the greatest so they were probably in the mood for some kind of distraction – and plenty of booing for me as I went in to sit among the substitutes.

A pat on the back coming off the field? I should have got a kick up the arse, but that was the beginning of me getting some amount of shit.

To make matters worse, a photographer took a picture of that exact moment. Fair dues to him for getting it – it was a brilliant picture – but it was no help to me when it was all over the papers the following day. If I'd even said to Justin after the match, 'I'm sorry I didn't shake your hand', it might have blown over, but I didn't. There was an awful atmosphere in the dressing room afterwards, and if things were going wrong before the game, it was diabolical afterwards.

When we got out of the Gaelic Grounds some of the players went to the back of the bus and the talk was simple enough: he's got to go. It was that quick.

7 March 2010: Carriganore, Training Session

Where does the time go?

Fourteen years ago I walked into a Waterford dressing room in Ballygunner, a raw teenager, and I'm still here.

In some ways it hasn't changed at all. You still have some lads coming in late, some lads covered with dust from the building sites, some lads in suits, shirts and ties. Slagging each other about work, women, new boots. It's the same soundtrack in dressing rooms all over the country.

In other ways it's completely different. That first night in 1996 I just got a phone call from Tony Mansfield, the senior manager, inviting me in. Nothing major. A few nights later I headed down with the Growler – Sean Daly – Paul Prendergast, Ollie Wilkinson and a couple of other Lismore lads to train. No bother, apart from one night the headlights went in the car and we drove from Waterford to Lismore in pitch dark.

Not now. These days, if a young player is in line to come on to the Waterford senior panel, he's screened by a doctor with a full series of tests to make sure he can take the training.

That's different. So is the approach to us, the over-thirties.

There's no point in flogging us around a field in January and February, so we're given a gym and stretching programme after Christmas and assessed regularly on our progress with it. Everything changes.

When I look around the dressing room before we head out to do the session now, I think of the faces that have moved on, the lads who have their feet up at home now watching EastEnders *instead of slogging through the mud with us here.*

Fergal Hartley has retired. A rock of a centre-back and a great man to have in the dressing room, not just for his leadership but for wearing some of the worst clothes in recorded history. The slacks and shirt Hartley would have on him would be stuck to him, or the jeans he'd be wearing would be an inch too short, showing plenty of sock. The fashionistas in the dressing room would give him plenty of it, and he'd give it back. Brian Flannery has packed it in too. A tough man to have at corner-back and smart enough with it.

Some of the older lads are still here. Tony Browne was in this dressing room before me and he's still here. He's always the last to come back every year and he'd tell you he wouldn't be training, but you'd know well that he was. You'd know he was working out on the treadmill for twenty or twenty-five minutes. He'd tell you he wouldn't be. But that's Tony for you. When he peels the shirt off he's not just fit, he's cut, as Eoin Kelly says.

Eoin and John Mullane are here, of course. The two tearaways are now experienced men, players the younger lads look up to. They've calmed down a lot since the days Mullane led us in a sing-song up in Antrim, belting out rebel songs, though every now and then they'll break out. One of the younger players was out with Eoin after a game in 2009 and finding the pace in the pub a bit hectic; I'd say he was nearly relieved he got hauled out by his father early that evening.

There are other changes. My first night training in Waterford in 1996 was in Ballygunner club, but this year the first session I was at was in Carriganore, the pitch Waterford Institute of Technology owns near the city, and the facilities are top class.

Down the other end of the dressing room you have the youngsters. The new breed. Different clothes, different music, different outlook. Guys like Tomás Ryan – and Noel Connors played in a Munster under-21 final last year: they know they're as good as anybody out there, no matter what county jersey they're wearing. They don't feel inferior to anyone, and they're right not to.

Of course, I know one of those youngsters better than most. My brother Maurice was only five or six when I first joined the Waterford senior hurling team. At one of those early sessions I remember lapping one or two of the older lads when we were doing rounds of the field, and they weren't a bit happy about it. Now I'm in danger of getting the same treatment from Maurice. I'm not a bit happy about it.

We get the call to go out. I pick up the stick and the helmet, but the question remains.

Where does the time go?

1

I was born in Cork – to the Cork supporters who'd be abusing me in Thurles or Páirc Uí Chaoimh I'd say that's a bit of a surprise – and I live in Dungarvan now. I've played hurling for Waterford all over the country, and we've travelled the world on team holidays, but only one place is home for me.

Lismore is still my home, the place that means the most to me. Most people who know of the town will know Lismore Castle, with its ivy-covered walls and manicured gardens, hanging over the Blackwater on your right as you cross the bridge into the town, but for me Lismore is far more than a tourist attraction. It's my favourite place in the world.

When I was growing up it was smaller, just a lovely little town, but it was a great place to grow up, a great place for kids. We did everything you might imagine – we'd head up to the castle gardens, though that was more for the people travelling through as part of their holidays, or we'd cycle out to the country.

We'd sneak into the golf course for a quick game, not

bothering with any small details like green fees. Sometimes we were caught, which probably explains why I never caused Tiger Woods any sleepless nights. When all else failed we were left with the strand for a dip; cold as it was, it had to be fairly slim pickings entertainment-wise if we were reduced to that. Still, myself and my pals often froze our way through an hour or two of diving there, convincing ourselves it wasn't that chilly, even as our teeth were chattering.

There was a hill near the houses that we used to play on, but when I was a kid I watched the diggers and machinery roll in, and it was levelled. After a while it became clear that the workers were building a hurling field there, which meant we had a place to practise almost on our doorstep.

It wasn't always the Munster hurling final or the All-Ireland we re-enacted there: we also played a lot of soccer – and on the hockey field near the primary school, though many a ball was canted onto the riverbank. (You'd have to be from Waterford to know that 'cant' means lose the ball. You wouldn't have to be a small boy to realize what a disaster that was.)

It was brilliant because you'd have a big crowd of lads there, lads you mightn't have known because they were from a different part of the town. We got to know each other – all Lismore lads together. It's not the biggest town in the country, but as a kid there'd still be lads you wouldn't know from the outlying roads or villages nearby. Playing those massive mixed matches was a help to us later – in Lismore CBS, for instance, or with the GAA club.

*

I'm the oldest in our family. I've two brothers, James and Maurice, and two sisters, Sharon and Pauline, and for the first couple of years we lived outside Lismore, where my mother and father, Mary and Brian, grew up, then moved into the town.

On my mother's side I have four aunts, and on my father's I have two uncles and two aunts, and I'm close to them all. But of all my relatives outside my immediate family, I was always very fond of my grandmother on my father's side when I was growing up. Any chance I could when I was a kid, I'd head out to her farm with my father and my uncle.

That usually meant Saturdays, and it was paradise. Her place was a couple of miles outside the town, and I'd be up early in the morning for the drive with Tom. We'd have a day working the farm – we might be cutting timber, feeding cattle, picking stones out of fields, testing cattle: all that farming work, we did it all, and we did it together. At least, I thought I did. As a small child I was probably more of a hindrance than a help to the two adults, but they always took me along with them and they always included me in whatever job they were doing. I can remember standing up on the tractor looking out over my uncle Tom's shoulder as he drove along. He'd be blasting out a song, I'd be joining in . . . it doesn't sound like much when you put it down like that but we were happy out, the lot of us.

Working like that with members of your family gives you a good work ethic for when you're older, which is good, but it's also enjoyable. Any boy wants to be out doing the same work as his father, and coming into my grandmother's house after a good day's physical work with him, my hands dirty, washing to have a bit of grub . . . those are great memories. My grandmother would usually throw on steaks for us and we'd sit down together for our dinner, and of course she'd be saying how much work I'd done and what a help I was to my father and my uncle. I loved it so much out there that when I got old enough I often strolled out the road on my own, three or four miles of a walk, did a day's work, then walked back into Lismore – and enjoyed every minute of it.

There'd even be the odd day I'd let on to be sick to get out there – my attitude was that the school and lessons would always be there, but a day you could steal to spend on the farm was a treat you couldn't always deny yourself. Heading out the road, I'd be lost in my own world at times, looking forward to seeing my grandmother, though I'd keep an eye out for the cars, just in case. I was lost in my own world, but I was never that far lost. Occasionally my aunt Joan's kids, Dan, Pat and Eoin, would come along – Eoin in particular was always giving out even then.

I'm joking: that cousin, Eoin Kelly, was an outstanding hurler even at that age; although he was five years younger than me I could see he was a major talent. Of course, to listen to him now you'd think all I did was bully him every time he came out to Lismore, but I was showing the city slicker the ropes. Honestly.

It was great to see the city boys come up to the country – it probably toughened them up a bit and created a very strong bond between us all, which you can still see when Eoin and I are on the field for Waterford.

As my grandmother got a bit older my aunt Breda who

lived with her was a fantastic help to her. My aunt Joan moved to Waterford, and my uncle Donal was in England for years, though he came back in the early eighties.

I'm very friendly with his kids, which isn't surprising given how tight I am to Donal. He's like my third brother, to be honest, more than an uncle. Going back the years he was always a great support – after an under-14 game he might slip me a five-pound note for a bag of chips. He wasn't the only one who had me playing professional hurling as a teenager. My grandmother would come and watch me – she always had her favourite spots as a spectator, the one corner of Cappoquin GAA field if we were playing there, for instance – and she was very decent. Good days and bad days, she'd flick a tenner out to me. That was me, playing for pay long before the GPA was ever heard of.

Later on, my grandmother wanted me to win the Waterford Sports Star Award, the Park Hotel award, and I swore I'd do it for her. I did, and though she wasn't around when I got it, she was there in spirit. Unfortunately, she passed away six or seven years ago, but I still have great memories – of her, of being out on her farm. Of all of us being together.

When we moved into Lismore town itself it was fantastic. Growing up in Parks Road, we wouldn't have had much. My father got some casual work but, like a lot of people in the Ireland of the eighties, he was often on the dole.

Anything my parents could give me they gave me.

As anyone who lived through the eighties will tell you, there wasn't a huge choice of things to do in Ireland, but as a small kid I was a big fan of the wrestling. Once Giant Haystacks came to the Lismore Hotel for a personal appearance, and I was mad keen to go and see him. It cost a fiver, though, which was a fair amount of money those days, and a stretch for my parents. My father got me the fiver somehow and I got to see Giant Haystacks, but the lengths my parents went to for me was the real treat. It sticks out in my mind that they knew I wanted to go and moved heaven and earth to get me there. I just hope they know how much I appreciate it to this day.

Most of the time when I wasn't meeting seven-foot wrestlers I spent outside, hurling away out on the streets, but there was the odd treat as well. I was lucky enough with our neighbours, the Colemans, who headed up to Fermoy nearly every Tuesday to swim and brought me along – a big highlight, because the alternative was to head down to the strand nearby with the lads, where the water was a lot less inviting.

There wasn't much in Lismore beyond playing soccer or hurling out on the street – or freezing down by the river, maybe – but it was a great community in Parks Road. My aunt Kathleen was across the street and my uncle Donal down the road; the rest of the family was all within twenty minutes' drive.

For holidays we might go down to Whiting Bay and swim for the day – heading abroad for a couple of weeks in the sun wasn't really an option for us – or the odd time Kathleen and Mikey would throw us into the car and spin down to Clonea beach with the family.

You can probably tell that family means everything to me.

I wouldn't have got anywhere without their support and I owe them an awful lot on both sides.

I've talked about my father's mother, but my mother's mother is a terrific woman as well. Her husband died very young – my mother hardly knew him – and she did an unbelievable job, rearing five daughters with no man in the house. She's ninety-two now but she's still able to enjoy the big matches.

My father's father was a massive man – they say I look like him – and while I don't remember him, I remember my father's uncle, because he always had a bag of Emerald sweets in his pocket and he'd load me up with them behind my father's back. I didn't need much persuading.

I'm proud of what I've done, coming from where I came from, but I couldn't give enough credit to my family, and my parents in particular. I often got a clip around the ear off the two of them, of course, but it was always deserved.

The hurling comes from my father's side of the family, though there'd be keen interest on my mother's side too.

My father played senior hurling for Waterford at full-back, and his big claim to fame is holding Limerick's Eamonn Cregan scoreless back in the seventies. Cregan was some hurler, so this is no small boast. Unfortunately Dad was in a serious car accident not long after that, which finished his inter-county career, though he played on for Ballysaggart after that.

When we came to Lismore he fell in with the club for a few years as well. He would have been known as a hard hurler, or maybe a very hard hurler, who spent a bit of time on the sidelines due to disciplinary complications. He missed a county final in the seventies through suspension, for instance, because of an incident in the semi-final.

My uncle Tom was different: he was a very skilful player and won the match the same day my father got the suspension.

To this day Tom is great to encourage me and gee me up – he'd ring me every night coming up to a big game, saying, 'How are the legs? How are you feeling? You'll do well Sunday.' A great support.

Due to work commitments, Tom left Lismore and went over to play for Roanmore in the city, and he won two county medals with them in 1989 and 1990. He'd have been a key player for them on the edge of the square. He marked Seamie Hannon in the old Fraher Field in a county final, and he did well, too. I can remember distinctly looking through the bars of the fence out at Tom during the game – I can still feel the metal bars on my forehead when I leaned forward to concentrate on the action, hoping Tom would get a score and, by God, he did.

At the final whistle, I ran on to the field to hug him, and he turned around to grab me. I was only nine or ten, but those are the memories, the things that inspired me to go on and try to improve myself. When you see your relatives do well you want to do the same.

That's the strength of the GAA. You've somebody who's a hero to everyone in his town, or his village, but five miles up the road nobody might have heard of him. That doesn't matter a damn to his own people, though. They know what he's done and he's a big man in his own place because of it.

My uncle Tom means a lot to me, and you can tell what

family means to him from one incident in particular. A couple of years ago my brother James was suspended – wrongly, I thought – by a Roanmore referee and Tom stood by James. He would hand back his county medals to Roanmore because he thought James had been wronged. James went on to play under-21s for Waterford.

My other uncle, Donal, who'd headed to England when he was young, was a very good soccer 'keeper. He got involved in hurling at club level and was very supportive of me from underage up. My mother's sisters' husbands, my uncles, have always been supportive, and her mother would ring me before matches.

In Lismore the lads know how to get a rise out of me: they'll start talking about Lismore men, and then they'll say my father is a pure Ballysaggart man. For the record, he's not. He's a pure Lismore man, like me. It's my club, it's always been my club, and it always will be my club. If you leave your club, you can't be a club man. No matter how it goes, good or bad, you always stick with your own – that's always been my attitude, even if other people think differently.

I was lucky as a kid in that I was very healthy. I don't remember a day that I was unwell, and my mother backs that up.

I was lucky with where I grew up too. In Parks Road there were a lot of kids around the same age. There were sixty-two houses on that road and Lismore got a lot of hurlers out of them.

According to my mother I was hard to get to primary school. Good enough to get as far as the gate, but not that keen to go any further to investigate what might be going on in the classrooms. A reluctant scholar, you might say.

I never had any problems with teachers and I don't think I caused many problems for them either. I was thrown out of class in primary one day because I asked a pal of mine – Michael 'The Chicken' Shanahan – a simple question. We were doing music and he happened to mention his flute and I said, in innocence, 'Miss, my flute is bigger than the Chicken's.' Cue pandemonium in the classroom. The teacher clearly thought my imagination was a little advanced for my age and we got to stand outside the classroom door for a while.

It was rare that I caused any trouble. The Chicken and I are still friends today, despite the trouble his flute caused me. I don't know where I'd be today without his support.

I was a bit of a trial to Mr O'Shea, another of our primary teachers, because he was big into music and I've no voice at all. Given what happened with the Chicken's flute you can guess that, from an early age, I didn't hold out much hope of a career as a musician.

The teacher I most respected in primary was definitely Sean Prendergast, and I suppose it's no coincidence that he was a mainstay of Lismore GAA club. He earned the respect of every kid in the school easily – he was just one of those people who commanded respect, immediately and naturally, through his personality; he gave everything to Lismore hurling, but he also got the best out of everybody in class. We were all determined to stay out of the 'black book' he kept. Anyone from Lismore will know what I'm talking about when I mention that: getting your name into Sean's black book was basically like having a judge enter your name on an offenders' register, and there was no appeal to a higher authority for a temporary release.

When all's said and done, though, I only had one subject in school: hurling.

2

As far back as I can remember I always had a hurley in my hand, growing up in Lismore. It was nothing but hurling in Parks Road. We were so mad for it we often played hurling on roller-skates. If your sister had good skates she'd have to keep an eye on them or she might see them on you as you flew up and down the road, roller-hurling.

I wouldn't say I was the best hurler starting off in school but I came on as I grew older and got more serious. We'd play in the schoolyard: the shed was one goal and a square on the wall the other, and it might be just ground hurling for the day: morning until evening without getting the ball into your hand, flaking it along the ground for hours at a time. We probably should have given the hockey a go, now that I think of it: we might have picked up an All-Ireland medal for Waterford.

Brother Dormer organized that, and what made it special was that he'd make sure we had a load of different jerseys. You had a fair cross-section of counties – and countries – flying around the yard: Kerry, Poland, Donegal, Tyrone. Places that had never heard of hurling gave great displays with the small ball in the Lismore schoolyard.

I started off in goal, oddly enough, because I was the youngest. After a year or so I got a bit bigger, came out the field and started to improve. I put a huge amount of that down to the influence of the likes of Sean Prendergast and Brother Dormer in primary school, John Heneghan and the principal Maurice Geary in secondary school. You couldn't overstate everything they did for us in those years, coaching, pointing out what you needed to do to get better. Everything. They could be tough to deal with – you'd get the odd thump if you deserved it – but they brought us on a lot.

As we got older we started to travel – to under-12 tournaments down in Clonmel, or up to Na Piarsaigh in Cork city for under-13/14. Big teams, big tournaments. That was a huge development for us, to be heading away from Lismore to places we didn't know anything about – where the accents were a bit strange!

We'd stay overnight with a local family, and that was a great experience, meeting people who were taking us into their homes and looking after us. Going away and coming up against different teams, different counties, toughened us up: just because they were hospitable to us at breakfast when we stayed overnight didn't mean they'd take it easy on us during a game. It was good for our confidence.

Of course, when Maurice Geary came in as a Waterford senior selector with Davy Fitzgerald he'd remind me of the days back in Lismore Secondary School – coming along the corridor and finding me at the door for messing, a quick poke on the shoulder as he'd go past. 'I didn't thump you hard enough, Dan,' he'd say, when he fell in with the senior team.

*

I came on as a hurler around ten, eleven, twelve. Sean Prendergast and Brother Dormer's tuition was getting through, and my touch improved. So did my accuracy. I began to notice that when we went away to the Clonmel tournament, or if we were up in Cork playing Na Piarsaigh, opposition mentors were shouting at their players about me, and putting good players in to mark me. That showed me I was getting somewhere, and then I got some more recognition: I played in Croke Park when I was twelve. Before the Offaly–Antrim All-Ireland semi-final back in 1989, Brendan Landers, Dave Bennett, Thomas 'Winger' Landers and myself of Lismore were in the under-12 mini-sevens half-time game.

A big occasion? Stop. My parents brought me up; they had two free tickets for the game. We went in and were togging off in Croke Park dressing rooms and putting on the little Offaly jerseys, shorts and socks. Then the jog out the tunnel on to the field – the same tunnel we'd been watching the previous year for the All-Ireland final and semi-final itself. It was out of this world. I couldn't tell you the first thing about the game we played, but one thing I remember clearly from the day is going up to Nicky English for his autograph after the second semi-final – Tipperary beat Galway in the game after Offaly–Antrim – but he didn't give it to me. You can even see it on TG4's *Laochra Gael* documentary about Nicky: you can see me running up to him and Nicky shrugging me off. I wasn't that upset about it – it was enough to be out on the Croke Park pitch – but it taught me one lesson: if someone's looking for some of your time, particularly a child, give it to them.

Some of the kids were asked back to play before the All-Ireland final, but I wasn't. What harm? I had the day out and the free gear and, which was more important, a taste of Croke Park, a look around on the day of a big game, and I wouldn't understate how important that was. Croke Park has changed a lot since then – it's a far more modern and attractive stadium now – but even then it was some arena. If you were up on Hill 16 you could probably see the cracks in the masonry, but out on the field, where we were, it was magic.

We were standing on holy ground, let's be honest. The ground we'd watch on television all summer, the one we'd wondered what it was like to play on, how the stands appeared when you looked up at them, looming over you like a cliff.

And then we were there. Twelve years of age and our studs were sinking into the turf of Croke Park, we were seeing the old pitch, with the uneven roll of the ground down by the Hill 16 end. And along with that, an inkling, maybe, that I might be able to survive at the top level.

The first actual game I can remember was probably a five-a-side in the schoolyard or Dick Ahearn's league in the field, and we had plenty of matches like that as small kids. Just a crowd of children running in a pack after the ball.

The first big game, though, was that Clonmel under-12 tournament I mentioned. There were two fields in Clonmel, and if you made the final you'd be on the main field; if you didn't you were stuck to the back field. We took a while to make progress, though, and we played a lot of games in the back field. It was like playing tennis at Wimbledon but never getting a sniff of Centre Court.

And names would float around. I remember one year there was a lot of talk about Babs Keating's nephew, but it just goes to show how sometimes advance intelligence is wasted. The adults with us would probably have been impressed to hear we'd be facing Babs's nephew, but we had no idea who Babs was. Or his nephew, come to that.

Then there were the Na Piarsaigh tournaments – that was where I first came across a young fella called Seán Óg Ó hAilpín, who obviously caught my eye immediately, the way he looked. I took even more notice of him because he was a serious opponent – big, strong, athletic. I knew I'd be seeing him again in a red jersey, not just the black and amber of his club. We wouldn't have chatted a lot then – you know what youngsters are like: they don't tend to have long conversations. The irony is that when we played against each other for Cork and Waterford in later years, I'd be in his ear the whole time, trying to put him off.

Our top rivals then were Dungarvan, but we had the better of it with them, usually. We had a good team coming up – we eventually made that main field in Clonmel – and we came good for the Féile na nGael. It's an under-14 competition that was a big deal then, and still is now. We won the Canon Fogarty All-Ireland B grade in it and went on to win the national Féile title at that level in 1988.

I was a sub on the team, and it's funny what has stayed with me, the odd incident that burned itself into my memory. Brother Dormer, who was involved with the club, said they'd send someone up to meet President Hillery before the final. I overheard Br Dormer say it was probably the only time I'd captain Lismore, so they'd send me.

I never forgot that. I was only a child, and you'd think it would run off me, but it stuck with me. People think I'm laid-back, and I am in a lot of ways, but to hear something like that – particularly when I wasn't meant to hear it – struck home. It inspired me and I captained Lismore for years afterwards.

At the same age as the Féile – under-14s – there's also the Tony Forrestal tournament at inter-county level. In Waterford there are trials between the eastern and western divisions, and you could get an idea of your level within the county – whether you were miles off the pace and were wasting your time, or whether you had some chance of making the grade. If you weren't good enough for the Tony Forrestal, for instance, it was the Sonny Walsh team, the lower grade, and I was lucky enough to play in both tournaments in different years.

It's usual to read about inter-county players that, as kids, they were prodigies who couldn't help scoring four goals a game, but I was a relatively slow developer. I was big and strong, but I grew and got stronger – a lot stronger – after fourteen, and my skill improved the stronger I got.

Another man whose skill improved alongside mine was Dave Bennett. I grew up with him in Lismore, and we were together all the way through school and underage teams. He was far more skilful than I was when we were kids – he insists on reminding me of that every time we meet up – but as I remind him, some of us grew up after that. And up. And up.

Along with Paul Flynn, Dave was probably one of the best strikers of the ball we had with Waterford, left or right, from play and frees, but he was harshly done by. A few of our managers seemed to see him as the first man to take off. Other lads had bigger names and stayed on when they should have been given the shepherd's crook, but he was the one who'd get pulled. Like Flynn, I think he could have stayed on for another year under Davy Fitzgerald but he didn't fancy it, and when he gave an interview the Christmas after the All-Ireland final criticizing Davy's tactics, I knew he was gone.

He's a great friend of mine, though I ended up cursing him a few times. On one team holiday we went to an amusement park in Orlando, Florida. Dave, Tom Feeney, Paul Flynn and myself went on this ride called the Hulk. The lads enjoyed it; I enjoyed getting off it at the end, a lot paler than I was at the start. Any time I meet either of them they remind me of the day the Hulk put manners on me.

In time other tournaments came into view, and by then I was making the top team in the county – under-16 tournaments with West Waterford, and minor hurling with the county. And I started to show. I scored 1–4 against Clare one day in Bansha, for instance, and my confidence started to build.

It helped that I was so big. Standing around six feet tall is an asset at senior level, so it obviously helped me in under-age games. It was also useful at inter-county minor level, a big step up from under-16 or under-14.

There was another big boost around that time – 1993 – when I was still playing under-16. The Lismore senior team got to the county semi-final against Roanmore and Sean Prendergast, who was managing the team, asked me to come along to training. I'd say he was just keeping his options open, but as the game progressed, it got tighter and tighter, and he sent me on with a few minutes to go at corner-forward to see if I could do anything.

It was intimidating: I was out against grown men who weren't inclined to make allowances for a youngster, but I got on the ball, and I won a 65 to tie the game up. With our last attack the ball broke in around the Roanmore full-back line. I stayed out, because I knew I was too light to mix it with the big men, and the ball rolled out to me, in oceans of space. I snapped it over the bar – I wasn't too far out – and the game was over on the puck-out.

There was another twist to the day. The lads were all about me, clapping me on the back and hugging me, when the game finished, but one of the opposition made sure he came over to me. It was my uncle Tom, who was Roanmore's top forward.

'Well done, Dan,' he said, and threw his arms around me.

Rare enough, to play in a county semi-final against your own uncle.

In the county final we played Passage – a miserable, wet day in Walsh Park. I got a bit of attention off the Passage defence after the semi-final, but I had plenty to mind me; Passage had a hardy team but the likes of the O'Sullivans and the Prendergasts on our side were every bit as tough.

We won the game, and the scoreline – eight points to seven – tells you everything about the quality of the game. The quality of my celebrations wasn't what it would be nowadays either, since I was only sixteen. Even at sixteen I marked some tough hurlers in Lismore – the likes of Seamus Prendergast, Dave Barry and James O'Connor and, by God, you would earn your score off them.

That was our last county title. We've been to the final a few times since, and it always seems to be Paul Flynn beating us on his own for Ballygunner, but we'll stick at it.

It's hard to explain to someone who's not a member of the GAA what your club means. To me it's everything – the lads who trained me and took me to games as a child, the lads who stand by me when I'm slagged off while playing for the county. The club is where you start and where you finish, and nothing would give me more pleasure than to win a county title with Lismore before I finish up playing.

I just hope we'll do it before the twentieth anniversary, or I'll be the only fella who was on the two teams!

We had decent minor teams in Waterford – we made three minor Munster finals in a row, though we got right hammerings from Cork in two of them. Getting to those Munster finals, in 1994, 1995 and 1996, was a big deal even if we didn't do ourselves justice. We were up against it, though, as Cork had very good minor teams at the time.

The manager Nicky Cashin's attitude helped. Going to Thurles for those Munster finals, he'd sit up at the top of the bus reading a book while we'd be nervous wrecks seeing the crowds. We were only children. What would have stood to us was that Waterford weren't actually making the senior final. You might think it would have benefited us to have home support, but I honestly think that if there had been thousands of Waterford fans in the Square, cheering our bus as we'd gone through, I'd have been sick with nerves. But Nicky would always remind us, 'Take it all in, lads, this is what you're trained for.'

When I say Cork were good I'm not kidding – they had the likes of Dónal Óg Cusack, Diarmuid O'Sullivan, Seán Óg Ó hAilpín, Dara Cott, Seanie Farrell, Timmy McCarthy and Joe Deane. I was on Seán Óg in one of those minor games and there wasn't much between us, but a lot of those names won All-Ireland senior medals later. That's what we were up against.

It was an early warning for me, though, in other ways. I remember in one of those Munster finals a few lads up on the terrace roaring abuse at me. Maybe they noticed me because I was the tallest on the team; I was certainly no worse than anyone else out there.

Derek McGrath of De La Salle was in the forwards with me and he came over at one stage. 'Don't mind those fucking fools, Dan,' he said to me. 'They're just a shower of drunks. Ignore them.'

We were all only young fellas together but that showed the class of Derek McGrath. I wasn't surprised when he trained De La Salle to win the All-Ireland colleges a couple of years ago. He was a leader all the way back then.

The preparation wasn't always at professional standard. It's fair to say I got away with a few things at minor level you wouldn't get away with now. We got tickets one time for the Irish Open at the K Club – me, my uncle Donal, his son

Brian and Michael 'the Chicken' Shanahan. That was the Saturday before we played Tipperary in the minor championship on the Wednesday night, but we went up anyway. Somebody's phone went off when Colin Montgomerie was lining up a shot, and Monty lost the head with him. Myself and the Chicken said we had too much respect for his putting to risk upsetting him, so we headed for the bar. Murphy's and Heineken were sponsoring the tournament and we enjoyed ourselves for the day – out every now and then for a sandwich, then back to the bar.

We fell back down the road – or we would have if we hadn't fallen asleep in the back of the car to Lismore. Straight into JR's for the night when we got back.

A few nights after, I had a stormer against Tipp, got a few points against them over in Fermoy, and I'd say some of the selectors knew I'd been out, but it wasn't that big of a deal. I shouldn't have done it, but I did. The worst of it – my biggest regret – was that I lost my brand-new Irish Open souvenir cap in JR's that night and all I picked up was a sick head on the Sunday.

There were better days. In school, for instance, we got to the Harty Cup final. Unless you know the Harty Cup, the senior colleges' hurling competition in Munster, and the traditions of the competition, you wouldn't understand what that means, or what it would mean to a small school like Lismore CBS. Getting to the Harty Cup final was huge for us in Lismore. We had a small school, and making a big game like that was some achievement. We were up against big names in schools hurling, the likes of the North Monastery – the Mon – or Midleton CBS.

When we played the Mon in the Harty semi-final in 1995 I was moved to corner-forward to keep me away from Seán Óg, who was their best defender. We wanted to upset their game plan, and it worked: I had 1–2 scored before they cottoned on to it and moved him back on me, which curtailed him from clearing ball further out the field – a great move from John Heneghan.

The plans didn't work as well in the final: we played Midleton CBS in Fermoy, and they had a good team – Mickey O'Connell, Joe Deane, Dónal Óg in goals. Many other Cork minors were playing, as well as another good hurler, Dara Cott. Deano beat us, though I got three goals myself.

It was good to have some positives from school, because it wasn't always the most enjoyable experience for me. I was no good at mechanical drawing or any of that – as my father said, I have two left hands – and to this day I'm no good with my hands apart from hurling. I was grand at English and so on. We had good teachers; Barra Connolly ran the library and we often called to his house, but that was because he was the only person around who had Sky Sports at home. Myself, Big John Begley and the Chicken practically moved in once a week – every Monday night we'd drop in to watch United v. Liverpool or whatever was on.

I had a couple of scrapes in school – like skiving off the odd day, nothing that threatened to get me suspended. I got a good Inter Cert, and while the Leaving Cert wasn't that bad, I failed maths, which was disappointing. I had thoughts of becoming a garda, which I couldn't pursue without maths. That might surprise you, but it was something I concentrated on that last year in school. The Celtic Tiger wasn't exactly roaring around Lismore and I felt it would be a good option for me. Maybe the hurling would help. But the maths let me down – otherwise I'd be writing this as Garda Shanahan, or Sergeant Shanahan, even, at this stage.

I did my best in school, but when I left in 1995 the work options weren't that great.

My grandmother's wasn't the only place I worked as a young lad. I often got a day's work off Sean O'Sullivan in Lismore and headed off with him to round up and dip sheep, shearing them and turning them. I'd fall in with Mattie Prender, too, for farm work. It was a good grounding in discipline and application, and showed me the importance of hard work, a lesson I've never forgotten.

My father went to Dave McGrath in the bacon factory when I left school, and he was good enough to give me a start. In all honesty, though, it's horrible work. I was essentially working in a slaughterhouse – I could be put to pulling out a pig's insides and throwing them into a bin. The smell alone would knock you out.

On another day I might have to go into a ten-foot curing tank and pull out bacon with a hook and stack it – I did that for a good while. Unpleasant? That wouldn't cover it. I did it before the break for lunch. After that I might have to go down to the 'kill', where I'd have to stun the pigs, cut their throats, rack and singe them. You put the pig up high and get a red-hot torch with flames coming out of it and singe off the bristles without burning the skin. I'd do some sweating after an hour of that.

At least it was a job, and they were good to me. I had plenty of friends there – John Casey, Pad Joe Reddy, Joss Farrell (God rest him), the Chicken, John Coughlan RIP, and Pat Ahern, not forgetting the ladies, Miriam and Karen. And I had as much craic as you'd have in any job. On a Monday morning, you might be raw with a hangover and get sent off to collect something from another part of the factory, only to go around the corner and get a belt of a pig's head.

If you've never seen a man wearing a pig's face when you're dying with a sick head, believe me, you haven't lived.

The best job was boning the animals, which was skilled, but with my two left hands that wasn't an option for me. Where I was, I'd start at six a.m. – five, coming up to Christmas – and maybe work until eight in the evening. The overtime was good – I had a few bob and was able to head out at the weekend. Not to mention that I'd have pork steaks, a few rashers and sausages for home. Good stuff for a growing boy.

One of the lads, Kevin Whelan, was put in charge of the packing and I moved into that part of it. It was good to have a job, but it was really money for drink, funding expeditions in the fleshpots of Lismore – The Red House, Koochie's and JR's.

On the other hand, the bacon factory was hard, physical work – and dangerous at times. We were messing one day and Alan 'Speedy' O'Donoghue slashed me by accident down at the 'kill' across the back of the fingers – I had to get stitches in that wound. Another day a pallet fell on the

Chicken – I didn't see it but I noticed him roaring with pain. I ran to him and got it off him somehow.

I was a bit embarrassed at times. The Waterford lads from the city might ask me, 'Where are you working?' and I wouldn't want to tell them. Some of them had very good jobs, so I had the eye out the whole time for something else.

I was mobile as well, which was something. I probably got into driving a bit later than a lot of lads around the place, but my father had a white Opel Kadett and he brought me out for a few lessons. Too bad he was the worst instructor I ever had in my life – 'You're not changing the gears right, you're revving the engine too much.' I had to get lessons off Noel Hennessy. I failed the test the first time but passed it the second time round. I hear fellas say now that it can help in the test if you're a good hurler. I've no idea if that is so but it certainly was no help to me when Waterford weren't winning Munster finals.

I was living at home but I was getting to an age where I was coming home late, and my mother would be saying, 'Where were you? Who were you with?' She was looking out for me more than anything else, of course, but eventually I had to move out.

At least there were compensations on the playing field.

3

Tony Mansfield, the Waterford senior hurling manager, gave me my senior debut in the National Hurling League in late 1995 or early 1996. It was a big day for me, though the main thing I remember now is that I marked a lad I'd share a dressing room with later.

It was in Thurles and Brian Flannery was the Tipperary corner-back, but the year after that he left Tipp and came to Waterford to work, falling in with Mount Sion and Waterford, eventually. There wasn't a dirty stroke in him but he could be cranky. One evening in the Fraher Field a few years later, Justin McCarthy asked us to do a drill – running out, head over heels in the grass, get up and sprint again. Flan shouted out, 'I came up here to play hurling, not to do head over heels on grass,' and he walked off. He had to apologize, but what about it? He wasn't the first and he certainly wasn't the last.

In 1996 I got the call to come training with the county senior hurlers, and that was clearly a ticket to the big-time. I chatted to my father about it and he said, 'Sure, give it a go.'

I was seventeen or eighteen, which is young to fall in with a club senior team, never mind a county team, but his attitude was, 'What's the worst that can happen? You can't hack it this year and you have to come back? You could go again next year when you're stronger.'

I'd been fine with the minors, and with Lismore CBS in the Harty Cup, but the senior county team was totally different. Before going training with them for the very first time I was nervous. Wicked nervous. I was going in to tog off with lads I'd been cheering for years. I had played against some of them at club level, and I'd seen how good they were. Senior inter-county means the very best of the best.

I was lucky enough that a few other lads from Lismore were on the selection, so I had company. I headed off down to Ballygunner for the first session with Sean Daly and Paul Prendergast, and that made a big difference for me, having the familiar faces there as well.

Not that they spared me. All I heard in the car down was, 'Ah, Dan, Bugsy [Byrne] will probably cut the head off you in the first minute of the backs-and-forwards, but don't mind that – he does it to everybody on their first evening.'

Nonsense, of course. At training the older lads – Damien Byrne, Stephen Frampton, Fergal Hartley, Ray Barry, Seanie Cullinane, all of them – couldn't have been nicer to me, but they were that bit older. I suppose I wasn't cheeky enough yet to be slagging them. I hung around with the Lismore lads, or one or two other young fellas who had been brought in. Like the blond kid from Mount Sion. Ken McGrath's first night at Waterford senior training was my first night as well, and you could tell immediately he was going to be a great player. I'd played with him all the way up on Waterford underage teams, and from his first inter-county training session, he played as though he was still playing under-14 in Mount Sion.

It's some laugh when you think about it; I just hopped into the car with the lads and went off to training. You didn't get medical clearance from anybody to play senior inter-county hurling then, and the thought of having to do so would have made the lads laugh.

When Maurice, my brother, was called on to the Waterford senior hurling panel in 2009 he was screened by medics to make sure he was able for the training physically. That's no harm, particularly after incidents like the death of the Tyrone footballer Cormac McAnallen from Sudden Adult Death Syndrome a few years ago, God rest him.

The training itself was fine. We had ball work, but we also did a lot of stamina work, which meant laps of the field. That was the in-thing at the time: laps of the field.

Then repeat. And repeat again.

That didn't bother me – I enjoyed training, always have, and at seventeen or eighteen, you're naturally fit as well. I was well able for those sessions.

I felt good as it came nearer to the championship game too; in one of the last sessions myself and Paul Prendergast lapped a few of the older lads, which showed me that I was able for senior inter-county, at least in terms of physical preparation. My parents were looking forward to the game hugely, and though I warned them that I wouldn't be starting, I think they were hoping I'd come on at some stage. To tell the truth, so was I.

I was disappointed with the championship itself, though. The selectors didn't start me in our first and only game, the Munster semi-final – there were no qualifiers or back door in 1996. We lost to Tipperary in Walsh Park by only three points, 1–14 to 1–11, though Paul Flynn got our goal from a free very late in the game to make the scoreline look respectable. What disappointed me most, though, was that they didn't put me on. The one thing I can remember is the Lismore lads looking after me that year, in particular Paul Prendergast who became a good friend of mine.

It's worth remembering that the build-up was totally different back then – it would have been in the papers, a bit of local radio, but there wouldn't have been much television coverage, and there was no Internet, really. Because of that, a fella had a chance to come in on the quiet, and the other team wouldn't have had much of an idea about him. Nowadays when a player makes his debut in the championship the other team already know about him; there are probably clips of him playing on YouTube, and there's a lot of chat on the Internet about what he does or doesn't do when he has the ball. Does he go for his own score or put the head down and run? There's practically an information overload these days.

It was totally different then. I was an unknown quantity, and I thought that if the selectors had put me on I might have offered something different to the team.

Ken McGrath made his debut that evening at wing-forward and scored a point, but he ran Tipperary ragged in the half-backs because they didn't know him or anything about him. That was the element of surprise in action, and I thought we could have doubled our return if they'd put me on. It was a letdown, sitting in the dugout in Walsh Park – which tells you something: nobody would seriously consider having a Munster championship game in Walsh Park now. Even with the dip in attendances in the last year or two, you'd still expect Waterford to draw well over twenty thousand for a Munster championship game, which Walsh Park could never hold.

Watching Tipperary pull away was depressing. They were the better team on the day, no question about that, but they weren't unbeatable. They had some fine players – John Leahy played, so did Cormac Bonnar and Declan Ryan – but they weren't streets ahead of us.

I suppose you'd have to say, too, that it wasn't a good sign from our players that a teenager just brought into training was lapping some of them a fortnight before the championship. It showed that physically they were off the pace, and now Clare were doing that famously savage training under Ger Loughnane and Mike McNamara, running up hills at seven o'clock in the morning before heading back to do a full training session on the field that evening. Every other county was aware of that and realized they'd have to see the Clare level of preparation – and raise it.

Even I could see, new as I was, that we'd have to up our game if we were going to take on these teams, let alone beat them. Clare were physically hard, toughened up by that training, which they'd been doing for years. It was all ahead of us.

That's no reflection on Tony Mansfield and his selectors: they put absolutely everything into it when they were there, but other teams – Clare and Limerick in particular, and Wexford, who won that year's All-Ireland – had brought the physical side of things to another level.

It was no surprise to me when the county board announced they were bringing in an outside trainer, Gerald McCarthy from Cork. I thought it was a good move and looked forward to 1997 as the season I'd make my debut in the Munster championship.

However, we didn't get off to the best start, me and Gerald. In fact, we had the worst start possible.

4

I knew there was some kind of problem the evening Gerald asked me to have a chat with him and his selectors in Dunhill GAA club early in 1997. I wasn't a cocky lad: I'd played a few league games towards the fag-end of 1996 – that was when the league was played before Christmas – and I hadn't set the world on fire, but I'd survived.

We'd just finished a training session that night in Dunhill – a dirty, rainy night, early in the year, the kind of night that makes you wonder what sense there is in running round and round a muddy field in pitch darkness – but we'd got through it, and after putting down a session like that, there's a sense of satisfaction: you've done your work.

We were having the craic in the dressing room afterwards when Gerald stuck his head round the door and asked me to come out for a chat. I joined him and his selectors, Shane Ahearne, Mossie Walsh and Greg Fives (who passed away a few years ago), in a small room elsewhere in the club, and I knew it wasn't going to be good news. Whether it was the lads' body language, or the sudden quiet in the room, I could tell.

Gerald got straight to the point. 'Dan, we don't think

you're prepared to give us the commitment we need,' he said. 'We're leaving you off the panel. We'll keep an eye on how you do with Lismore and we'll be in touch if we want you to come back.'

I was stunned but not surprised, if that makes any sense. Earlier that day I'd played a soccer match with Lismore – I liked to think of myself as a handy striker, despite a lot of circumstantial evidence to the contrary – before coming out to train with the county hurlers. The soccer club were stuck and needed a dig-out, and I didn't want to let down a bunch of local lads – lads who were also my pals. I headed up, played the match, didn't over-exert myself between the lines, and went to training.

Obviously someone was trying to be helpful and tipped the selectors off.

I went back into the dressing room, gathered up my gear and headed home. I didn't tell any of the other lads: I was too embarrassed. When I got in I told my father and got an earful from him as well, particularly when he heard the reason I'd been dropped.

Gone, and all my own fault. Years of effort down the tube for a soccer match that nobody else remembers. Through acting the goat I'd lost my chance to nail down a place on the Waterford team. It wasn't that Gerald was some kind of zealot still following the spirit of the Ban, or anti-soccer, but he was right. If a fella was off playing soccer when he was supposed to be getting ready to train for his county then he wasn't going to be able to train to the fullest extent. And if that was the case, he wasn't taking it seriously enough. I deserved to be dropped. If it happened nowadays the manager wouldn't have to drop the player: the other panellists would tell him to pack his bags with no prompting.

Gerald McCarthy was a very good coach – very good on the skills of the game, very good in one-to-one coaching. He was a legend of the game and had won All-Irelands as a player and a coach with Cork. He'd seen it all.

And because he'd seen it all, I suppose he felt he had to put down a marker when it came to discipline on the Waterford team. I know well he didn't drop me because he had a personal issue with me; he dropped me because he felt I was immature, and because I was immature I couldn't be relied upon to give the commitment.

No matter what I had to offer as a player, if I didn't give the commitment to training I wouldn't be ready physically or mentally when it came time to deliver in the championship. I understand that now, of course, but it wasn't much consolation to me when I was dropped from the panel in 1997.

Dropping me probably had the effect that Gerald wanted on the rest of the panel. The other players probably thought, *He'll get rid of anybody he wants, no messing around.*

That was needed. As I said, I'd lapped players the previous season in training, which showed the improvement that was needed in the team – and the job Gerald had on his hands.

Changing the attitudes of players is a slow thing for a manager. That's not the same thing as changing their personalities – as the saying goes, some players need an arm around the shoulders to get the best out of them, and others need a kick up the arse. That doesn't change: it's just the way people are built.

But getting players to take things seriously – their diet, their time-keeping, their discipline on and off the field, their option-taking during matches, all of that stuff: those are things that you can change. It just takes time. And, as I found out, some fellas have to be sacrificed along the way.

They didn't get in touch, so I was left moping away for the year down in Lismore. Literally. I didn't even go to watch Waterford in the championship that year because I couldn't face it.

They went up to Thurles and lost to Limerick, and the story wasn't that different from Tipp in Walsh Park the previous year. The difference was six points at the end, but Waterford let in a couple of soft goals to help Limerick along. I was stuck at home, sitting on the couch.

It's only now that that really sinks in – the fact that I lost a year of my career through my own stupidity. It's bad enough if you have a serious injury, or even if you have to go abroad to work, but when you cock it up yourself, it's even harder to take. I just wondered, Why the hell did I do that?

Nearing the end of my inter-county career, I took a lot of care with my diet and training. I knew at that point that there weren't a lot of games left, let alone a lot of years, so I prepared myself as best I could for every game that came along. I also looked back on 1997 with plenty of regrets.

There were some consolations around that time. Myself and the lads were messing around one beautiful sunny summer's day at Clonea strand when I spotted three women looking at us. Now, at the time I was focused on the hurling, so I didn't think much of it, but we stayed over in Dungarvan that evening and I met one of them, a blonde, in Davitt's nightclub later that evening: Colette.

I walked her home and she put me up in her parents' house – in a spare bedroom, I might add – but when I woke up the next morning I slipped away out the road and back to Lismore. Of course, my mother asked me where I stayed, and I said Dungarvan. Which was true enough.

Colette and I stayed in touch and eventually we got together. Her family are terrific people, the nicest you could meet: Bernie and Monnie welcomed me into the house like I was their own the first time I met them, and they still do – I couldn't have met two nicer people. So did her eight sisters and two brothers.

It took my father and mother a while to get used to Colette, with me being the oldest – a mammy's boy, I suppose – but they're mad about her now. At this stage if I ever said something bad about Colette my own mother would take the head off me.

We've been together since. Like any couple we've had our ups and downs, but certainly the biggest high came with the arrival of Chloe in 1999 – which I'll tell you about a little later.

Late in 1997 I got a phone call from Gerald McCarthy. Or, rather, my parents did. I was out. When I got home they told me he'd rung and I was half thinking he wouldn't bother ringing back, but they told me to cop myself on.

He rang back. We chatted. He asked me to come back on the Waterford panel for 1998. 'As far as I'm concerned, 1997 is water under the bridge, Dan,' he said.

'Same here, Gerald,' I said.

I was delighted to get another chance, but I was also determined. There was no way I'd leave 1998 behind me after the year I'd missed out on.

5

Of course, just because Gerald and I had decided to forget my soccer career with Lismore, it didn't mean the other lads on the panel were going to leave it lie. Hey, I'd have been exactly the same in their shoes.

The first night at training Brian Greene and Micheál 'Haulie' White looked up when I came in. 'Well, Dan,' they said, with shock on their faces, 'no soccer match this morning?'

I could live with that.

When I came back on to the team Flynn was still one of the mainstays scoring-wise, but the real leaders were the likes of Seanie Cullinane and Fergal Hartley. People might wonder why Paul Flynn wasn't more of a leader. In effect he was, though: he mightn't have been roaring and shouting in the dressing room, or showing the younger lads the way to do things by leading the team in laps of the field, but he carried them for years in terms of scoring. By default he was one of the most important men we had in games. In training . . . not so much.

He usually spent his time at the back of the pack, particularly if we were doing the heavy physical stuff. I often spent the session alongside him, chatting to him, encouraging him, trying to drive him on. The running came easily to me, but he hated training. Hated it.

The irony was that he had a serious turn of pace; if he'd minded himself a bit better it would have been a fair weapon to have in his back pocket when it came to the championship. As it was, he didn't lack ammunition. The skill that Flynn had was incredible. If he took penalties in training, the backs – tough men – would be nervous, he had so much power in his shot. The goal he scored against Cork in the 2004 Munster final? I often saw him do that in training – put huge topspin on the ball and get it to dip on to or just under the crossbar as it came in. He could do anything with the ball: any way it came at him, he'd control it – kill it dead on his hurley – and any angle he was at, he was able to find the target.

Flynner's a hard man to know. I'm good friends with him but he takes time to figure out. If he doesn't like you then he doesn't like you, and in fairness, he doesn't like a good few people. If he likes you it's different – he's great company. If you have something he likes – a nice top in the dressing room, maybe – he'll take it off you.

When I came on to the panel I looked up to the likes of Flynn, and myself, him and Eoin Kelly would be in the same group in training. Eventually Justin broke up that group – maybe he thought we weren't putting in the effort, though we were.

*

Seanie Cullinane was our Rock – long before Diarmuid O'Sullivan collected that nickname up in Cork. In club games I had a fair few run-ins with him and he's not a man you'd enjoy meeting if you were flying towards the opposition goal.

In 1998, he led by example on and off the field. The training he put in for Gerald was unbelievable: he'd take off on nights we weren't in Fraher Field or Walsh Park and run for miles around the woods out by Passage. In the games he gave fantastic protection to Brendan Landers behind him, he encouraged the rest of the defence and generally held things together. He was disappointed not to win the All-Star for full-back in 1998, and I felt he was right to be: he was the best full-back around that year.

Hartley was another great leader, an outstanding figurehead. He was one of the top centre-backs in the game so he could do his own job as well as anyone around, but he'd take the fight to the opposition as well. If lads were in trouble, they could count on Hartley piling in to back them up. It was a different matter playing against him in club games: with Ballygunner, he was inclined to get into your head, shouting, 'Come on the Gunner,' when you'd be trying to concentrate.

On the negative side – negative when it came to physical exhaustion, that is – I'd timed my return perfectly, just in time for the new regime. After years of doing the kind of casual training that all counties did – a few laps of the field, a few sprints – we had caught up with everybody else, and we definitely trained harder in 1998.

There was one county to blame for that: Clare. We'd heard all the stories – that Clare were out training at seven o'clock in the morning, that they'd train twice a day, that the sessions were so brutal the players' families were banned from coming to them in Cusack Park for fear of seeing and hearing the abuse their sons and brothers were put through. It worked for them in that they won two All-Ireland titles in 1995 and 1997, and they might have won one or two more, given they were still getting to All-Ireland finals in 2002 and semi-finals in 2005.

But there were implications and consequences for other teams. You had to reach Clare's base level of fitness to compete, and even though they faded as a force, you couldn't turn the clock back to the old, pre-Clare days of training. That level of professionalism and all it implied – drinking nothing but water for six months of the year, having your urine tested every morning – was here to stay.

In 1998, we had our own secret training regime: the sand dunes out in Tramore. When people think of Tramore they probably associate it with a nice stroll along the prom, or a bag of chips up in the Beach Grill or Cunningham's, but when we heard the word 'Tramore', we thought, *Torture*.

Shane Ahearne, one of Gerald's selectors, brought in the training circuit in Tramore. You had to run down to the dunes from our starting point outside the town, which was a distance of two or three miles, then continue up to the Baldy Man on top of the dunes. The effect this had was unbelievable. Players would be getting sick all around the Baldy Man when they got up there. The only good news for them was that on the run back down through the dunes they'd have nothing to bring up. Or on the run back up again.

You'd go through that two or three times. Then, worst of all, when your legs were like jelly and you were feeling fairly light-headed, you'd have to jog back to the start and do a hurling session. It was savage punishment. Hard? Our feet would be sinking into the sand, and we'd have to drag ourselves out. Every step was a struggle. We were all nearly collapsing, trying to get oxygen into our lungs. There was vomit everywhere we looked. Repeat that once a week for a few months, and you'll have a fair idea of what we were going through in the early part of 1998.

Why did we do it? It wasn't just a case of doing what Gerald and the selectors wanted us to do, though that kind of discipline was part of it – if you obeyed orders in training without question, you'd do the same in a game when they told you to switch positions. There was more to it than that, and we were aware of it even as we were doing it.

First, as a training regime it was completely different from what we'd been doing, and the benefit went beyond improving our stamina and endurance. We were growing stronger in mind. Training like that made us ready for the championship, ready for the questions we'd ask ourselves at around five to five on a warm summer Sunday in Semple Stadium. *Can I win that ball? Can I chase my man down and get the block in? Can I break the tackle and get in my shot? Can I just keep going to the end?* After a spring of those training sessions, we knew we could answer those questions. We knew we were able for the best of them – and we got the proof of it even earlier than the championship when we reached the league final that year against Cork.

The single most important thing about the training, though, was that everybody bought into it. There was no complaining, no whingeing – everybody did it, and we did it together. That hadn't always been the case with Waterford teams. A couple of years before I'd joined the panel, there had been occasions when players from Mount Sion, say, might go and play a challenge game with the club rather than train with the county team.

That attitude was gone, thanks to 1998 and Tramore. There were no cliques, no groups. Shane Ahearne and the management team helped with that: for instance, Shane made sure that we went around the Tramore circuit in twos, so we always had somebody with us to encourage us if we were struggling. It built team spirit without the need for any big meetings or weekends away. It happened naturally. To me, that's the only way you can get a team to gel anyway – naturally. Fellas won't trust each other just on a manager's say-so. They have to decide that for themselves.

I found I could do the training, but I was often alongside someone like 'Haulie' White, and he found it harder. I'd almost have to carry him up the hill, and there were other lads like that. You had to wait for them to be sure they'd get to the top, and that made the bond stronger.

For all of that, it's difficult to explain to people how hard it was. No matter how fit you were, or how fit you thought you were – or how fit you thought the other lads were – you'd find out about yourself when you were puking your sandwiches on to the sand in the dunes.

Tramore was non-negotiable. It was the base level, the minimum you had to do to be considered for the team. That was another building block for us: if you didn't do the training you wouldn't be on the team.

Gerald brought in something else that year, which added to the discipline: the Nutron diet. People have probably forgotten about that now, but it was all the rage because Offaly had won the Leinster football championship the year before and credited the diet with getting them fitter.

We had to give a blood sample at a centre in Waterford, which was tested at a lab in England. They worked out from that sample the foods each of us needed to eat to get the most from our training sessions, and which foods didn't suit us. One fella might be told to lay off potatoes and coffee, another that he could eat all the potatoes and drink all the coffee he wanted.

My feeling was that it suited heavy players – if you needed to lose weight it would drop off you: most fellas were told to stop eating bread or potatoes or pasta, while junk food and beer were strictly forbidden. It was inevitable that you'd lose weight, particularly with the training we were doing. Gary Gater was on the panel that year and lost a load of weight; so did the likes of Fergal Hartley and Sean Cullinane. They got very strong as a result. Sean, in fact, was a walking advertisement for the whole thing: he'd never looked fitter in his life, I'd say, and he was always a good man to train.

It helped the players mentally, too, because it sent a message to everyone that they were professional sportspeople. We felt we were taking it seriously: we were told what to eat and drink, so we worked hard at our preparation and training. One thing fed another.

My blood sample suggested I should keep off white bread, which I did, after a struggle, and chocolate, which I did – after a desperate struggle. I was a fairly committed fan of a bar of chocolate during the day, but I managed to give it up.

Drink-wise, I was told to stay away from beer. We were told we could maybe have a bottle of cider instead of a pint of Guinness, or a vodka and white. You'd get drunk a lot quicker on vodka, but that's another story. You can tell how seriously we were taking it when we were even looking into how fattening our drinks were.

There were times in the dressing rooms in Fraher Field or Walsh Park when lads would be arguing about how to cook rice, whether you let it simmer for five or ten minutes, or whether you should throw butter in on top of it when it was done for a bit of taste, and someone else would say that was cheating because the butter was fattening . . . I heard a lot of strange conversations in dressing rooms over the years, but the debates on how to cook rice were some of the weirdest.

We weren't just left on our own to get on with the diet: I had to go into Waterford to the Nutron clinic where I'd be weighed and my blood tested. And again, every fella did it, selectors included. Some of us were in fairly good shape anyway but we still did it – and you felt that much stronger because of it. We were stronger in body, stronger in mind. We were stronger as a team.

*

Between all of that training and preparation, we were ready for Tipperary at Páirc Uí Chaoimh in the Munster semi-final. They had been in the All-Ireland final the previous year and had only lost when John Leahy missed a goal chance late on against Clare. They were a good team, strong and experienced, and they were entitled to be favourites.

But we had a secret weapon: our self-belief. We had gone through a ferocious regime of training and we knew we'd be fitter than them. The fact that they were the favourites didn't bother us in the slightest.

I was marking Conal Bonnar that day, and I was happy to be on him, compared to some of the other Tipp backs. He was a fine hurler: he'd hurl away against you and concentrate on the ball, rather than trying to cut the head off you. In the corners Tipperary had the likes of Paul Shelley and Michael Ryan, and they could cut you in two – if they could catch you. But nobody caught Paul Flynn that day. He was the man in Páirc Uí Chaoimh: he tore the Tipp full-back line to pieces. We were good enough on the day, even though it was close enough towards the end, but he made the difference. Flynn had suffered through the training in Tramore, but he showed the benefits of it that day.

With time running out I got the last point – not an epic score by any means; the ball just came to me in space and I popped it over the bar. The final whistle went soon afterwards. Greg Fives ran out from the sideline to me, lifting me up in the air.

I was roaring up into the sky, I was so happy. The previous year I'd had to pack my gear into a bag in Dunhill and head back to Lismore with my tail between my legs, and now we were in a Munster final. It had been nine years since Waterford had made it to a provincial decider, so we celebrated fairly well when we got back over Youghal Bridge.

I was still living at home but I headed on to Waterford with the boys: Muldoon's for the evening, then on to the house Flynn was renting out in Ballygunner. Partying all night and breakfast with the sun coming up, a fine greasy fry with the Nutron diet put on the shelf for twenty-four hours.

And a Munster final to come.

6

We were facing Clare in that Munster final, and the annoying thing about Clare wasn't that they were top dogs when I came on to the team back in the nineties: it was the fact that for years they hadn't been much better than ourselves. All the way up through the decades they hadn't much more than we had to shout about – and maybe winning an All-Ireland in the sixties, as we had, meant we were entitled to look down on them, if anything.

Coming into 1992, the future looked pretty good for us. Tony Browne led Waterford to the under-21 All-Ireland title, beating Clare along the way. Flynn popped up as a minor to help them over the line in the replay of the All-Ireland against Offaly – and there was no doubt which county was going places.

Fast forward five years and one of those counties had picked up two All-Irelands. Eighteen years on, the other is still searching for that particular title.

That's us. How did it happen?

To me, it's fairly obvious. Look at who Clare had on the line when they were at their best. Ger Loughnane, Tony

Considine and Mike McNamara were regarded by everyone as the holy trinity of management when they won the All-Ireland, but I don't think there's much doubt who the top man was.

When Tony Considine became manager of Clare he never saw eye to eye with Davy Fitzgerald and left fairly quickly. To me, that doesn't do much for Tony's credibility when it comes to passing comments on people in the paper and on the radio. Mike McNamara left the manager's job in Clare as well when his own players wouldn't play for him, and I couldn't really say I was surprised. In 2007 I was on the Munster Railway Cup team and he was in charge of it, and I could see he'd be hard to deal with – a rough manner with the players.

I got on well enough with him at that time and he often came over to shake my hand after that, but there's a hell of a difference between meeting up with a manager for an hour before a Railway Cup game and spending months listening to him as you run around a field in the rain during winter. You wouldn't be long looking for a divorce there if the differences between you are too big.

Ger Loughnane made the big difference to Clare. He was the focal point of our clashes with them in the Munster final in 1998. This was a Munster hurling final and you'd think the whole place would be following the action on the field, but at times I knew people were only looking at Loughnane to see what he'd do.

You can see what he's like even today, the way he analyses games on television: he mixes the passion that he must have had in the dressing room before games with the calm you need to pick out what's going right or wrong in a match. I've nothing but respect for him, even if Clare did beat us in 1998.

I have huge respect for Clare in general. They came from nowhere, really, to win two All-Irelands, and when I see the emphasis counties put now on underage success, I have even more respect for them because they didn't have huge talent coming through from their minors and under-21s at that time.

On top of that, they didn't have naturally gifted hurlers. They had outstanding defenders in the Lohans and Seanie McMahon, but in real terms they only had one forward in Jamesie O'Connor. He was outstanding, but he often had to fill in at midfield as well alongside Ollie Baker. (My main memory of Ollie is from 1998, when I bumped into him around the middle of the field and he threw a dig at me, adding, 'What are you looking at, you ugly fucker?' or something along those lines, the big eyes coming out of his head. You wouldn't forget that in a hurry.)

The funny thing is that while people were happy to see Clare win in 1995, ending eighty-one years for them without an All-Ireland, they couldn't wait to see Clare get beaten after that. The underdogs had come good and it was romantic, but then people got jealous of what they'd achieved, pure and simple. Then, in 1997 and 1998, I think they started finding it harder to get past the other teams and relied on their strength and aggression more and more.

They were never an attractive team to watch, but they definitely became more inclined to grind teams down as the years rolled on. It suited them to get into a dogfight with their opponents. It suited us to have a shoot-out, pure and simple. Developing the attitude for a dogfight is easy. When you're playing in the Munster or the All-Ireland championship, you have to hate the fella you're marking. That might sound strange, but it's true. I'd find it very hard to hate anyone – I'd just want to go out and hurl – but you could tell when you walked up to shake hands with the Clare lads before a championship match that they were ready for war.

The other side of winning those two All-Irelands was that Clare had fantastic experience. They didn't panic. They always reckoned they had a chance. In 2002, when we played them in the All-Ireland semi-final, we flew into a lead and Eoin was beating them on his own, but they stayed calm and reeled us in eventually.

But let's rewind. Against Clare in that Munster final in 1998, I felt no pressure. A player who's around twenty years of age, as I was then, doesn't have responsibilities. Such a young player is often a student or maybe has a casual job that he won't shed any tears about jacking in when the time comes. There are no outside elements to distract him from focusing on the game.

A player who's thirty years of age, though, probably has a mortgage, maybe a child, a job that carries a bit of pressure. He's not going to be facing into a game the same way as the lad who's ten years younger. I know myself I'd feel the pressure a lot more nowadays, and I understand how the younger lads on the team feel; sometimes I think it'd be nice to have that kind of freedom nowadays, but the trade-off is that I can draw on experience they don't have.

In 1998 we had both. We had players who could mix it

with you physically it if they wanted to, and we had others who could play hurling with you all day long. Most strong teams do.

I felt good going into the Munster final. I was marking Brian Greene most nights in training, and he was a serious player, with a huge burst of speed. If I could get the better of him in any way, I knew I was doing well. There were great personalities on the team as well – Seanie Cullinane, Fergal Hartley and Stephen Frampton had been there for years. They were strong guys in the dressing room, and when they had anything to say – about the opposition, about the referee – we all listened. I haven't changed in that regard: even today, if a young fella talks, I listen. Nobody knows it all.

Gerald was very good in the run-up to the Munster final. He had played in a good half-dozen provincial finals himself, and had trained teams to win them, so he knew the drill inside out. His coaching preparation was fantastic, really excellent. We focused completely on hurling drills in the week before, rather than any physical stuff, and he told us to go out and enjoy ourselves.

That mightn't sound like a complicated game plan, but he was responding to what he had. He'd have been well aware that a lot of lads, like me, hadn't played in such a big game in our careers up to that point. There was no sense in overloading us with details before the game and running the risk of lads freezing.

On the morning of the game the bus collected us in Dungarvan and we stopped on the way up to Thurles for a chat and a cup of tea, a quick puck-around. It sinks in a little then that the next time the bus stops you're going to be walking into Semple Stadium for the Munster final.

You have to remember something: a Munster final in Thurles is one of the biggest days in Irish sport, no matter what the year is, no matter who the teams are. We weren't used to it. The lads left on the team who'd been in the 1989 Munster final had played that game in Cork, so when we came around the corner in Thurles and headed into the Square, it was some sight.

There were thousands of Waterford people – and Clare people, naturally – all over the place, milling in and out of the hotels and pubs, slagging each other, drinking, buying and selling tickets. At occasions like that people say the atmosphere is electric and it sounds like a cliché, but when the bus rolled into that scene we felt it. There was a crackle in the air.

The Waterford supporters saw us and ran over, hammering on the sides of the bus, cheering us – and these were lads I'd known from Lismore, lads I'd sat next to in school or gone to games with, and there they were in their white and blue, screaming in the windows at us. Just to be on the bus, to experience that, was unforgettable. Incredible.

It made me extremely nervous. I began to understand what was at stake: *Christ, this is fairly serious. We're playing the All-Ireland champions from two of the previous three years. It's really happening.*

If people could have looked into the dressing room before that Munster final, though, they'd have been surprised.

There was no banging of hurleys on the table, no screaming at fellas to go out and die for the jersey, nobody taking the door off the hinges on the way out. It was a very calm scene, with Gerald and the selectors focusing on players individually and reminding them of the particular jobs they had to do.

Usually if Gerald was angry with a player he'd let him know – he had no problem shouting at anyone in the normal run of things, but a Munster final isn't the normal run of things. That day it was more about getting us focused. When a twenty-year-old is facing the biggest seventy minutes of his playing career, his mind has to be right: the first ball, the first touch. Ignore the crowd. The next ball, the next touch. Bit by bit, second by second. The game doesn't happen all at once. It happens in little bits, in chunks. The trick is to manage them.

Gerald would encourage us, not roar and shout, and I was encouraged anyway, sitting next to Paul Flynn, like I usually did. Then again, being next to Flynn would relax anyone. I'd say he never felt nervous in his life.

I was wing-forward, marking Anthony Daly, and I fancied my chances before the game. Daly was a great warrior for Clare and an outstanding captain, but while he wasn't coming to the end of his career at that stage, I was thinking that maybe he hadn't marked a fella like me before, with a bit more power than him, a bit more pace. I was a couple of inches taller than Daly and was convinced I was faster. Clare had played Cork in the Munster semi-final when he'd marked Seanie McGrath, a very different player from me.

That was my level of confidence in the dressing room but

out on the field it was different. The crowd, the parade, the occasion . . . It was another level up from the semi-final.

I was intimidated going up to shake Daly's hand, absolutely. No question about that. But you can't show an opponent you're intimidated at any level of the game: if an inter-county defender thinks you're nervous of marking him he'll stand down on top of you without a thought. You'll be mincemeat.

Before the ball was even thrown in I got a rap off him, but that was fine. This is the Munster championship we're talking about – I'd nearly be surprised if I didn't get a rap. Not getting one would have put me off.

We survived the first half: once the ball was thrown in it was just another game of hurling, and we didn't freeze. I was happy enough with how I played. I ended with three points and we broke even in most sectors but Clare, the bookies' favourites, took a strong lead in the second half, and looked to be coming with their winning burst at just the right time.

Myself and Daly had a bit of banter in the second half, when they were getting on top; Daly was a good man to talk at the best of times, and given that they looked like collecting another Munster title, you'd call that the best of times. He wouldn't shut up, so eventually I said to him after I scored a point, 'It's not Seanie McGrath you're marking now, boy.'

Daly came back: 'No, you're a lot fucking uglier.'

Not a bad response, particularly in the heat of a Munster final.

I felt I had the beating of Daly, and at that age I didn't worry about my opponent: that's the advantage of youth.

But it wasn't him that was the problem. If I got round him I had Frank Lohan coming out to meet me from corner-back, and if I managed to pass him and head for goal I had Brian Lohan to deal with. One after the other. There was a lot more to worry about than just Daly.

They had great players on that Clare team. Tough men. You could see how they'd won two All-Irelands, because there was no going back in them. They were the best in the business at that time.

But we had tough men, too, and we came back, and Paul Flynn played a huge part in that. For a player so good it's funny that he never got the recognition he deserved. He carried Waterford for years until a few new players came in to help out – he was under serious pressure to produce all the time for Waterford and he did, nearly all the time. And he kept us in the game that day, particularly with the frees. With a couple of minutes left he had a free in front of goal.

There were three points in it and there were no doubts about Flynn's intentions, whether up in the terraces or on the Clare goal-line. He eyed the ball and eyed the goal, and it was obvious that he was going to go for it.

Our backs would admit that they dreaded facing Flynn for penalties and 21-metre frees when it came time for him to practise at training; they'd be shaking on the line as he lined them up, and with good reason. I genuinely believe I've never seen anyone hit the ball as hard as him. Clare lined the goal for that free. As he came up to lift the ball, I prayed, *Paul, please, just stick it.*

And he did. When the net billowed, he did his run around Thurles with the arms out like an aeroplane. Draw.

We had a chance to win the match with the last puck of the game, a free, out in the middle of the field. I had one hundred per cent confidence in Flynn that he'd score it, and he struck it beautifully, but it just curled away and dropped wide. It must have been the guts of a hundred metres out, and I watched it tail away from the goal at the very last second.

Afterwards there were a few suggestions that maybe Tony Browne should have taken it, because he was on fire as well in midfield, but I didn't think so. Flynn was the man: he'd just buried the goal, and he had the confidence up.

When the ball was pucked out, the referee blew the whistle. We were heading for a replay.

Afterwards I felt disappointed. We made all the right noises about finishing the stronger side and having the initiative for the replay, but the reality was we knew we'd missed a great chance. It's always hard for the underdog to come back and do it all over again.

As it was, we probably made it harder for ourselves. We went for a few drinks after the game that night, and the refreshments probably came against us in the replay because a few of us stayed out the next day as well.

The Tour de France was coming through Dungarvan on the Monday and four or five of us were on the beer that day, inside Tommy Power's and Paddy Foley's in the town. On the lash. That was part of the scene – after a big championship game we'd head out and there'd be people coming up to put drink in front of me, saying, 'You got three points off Anthony Daly, go on, have a pint.' We were young, we didn't have our heads screwed on . . . The long and the short of it was that the four or five of us were in a bit of trouble when we got to training on the Tuesday night.

The selectors weren't happy and they let us know about it, but they didn't make a huge deal of it, which was probably the right approach as we only had a couple of days to get right for the replay.

In our defence we probably felt we'd get away with it, that we'd be well able to drive it on the following weekend, that it wouldn't affect us because we were young, fit and healthy. We found out the opposite the following Sunday, though.

That Tour de France caused suffering to more than the lads who cycled it.

We were conscious there'd be a backlash from Clare. Anthony Kirwan had scored two great goals off Brian Lohan, and I'd got three points off Daly. Flynn had got a rake of scores off Frank Lohan, Brian Greene had kept Jamesie O'Connor quiet . . . We knew they weren't going to take that lying down.

I wouldn't say we were well warned but the selectors had drummed into us the whole week that Clare were gunning for us – that they were disappointed with the way the game had gone for them, and that they were going to put down a marker. We were told to expect a battle because Clare were coming to Thurles to go to war with us. We weren't going to roll over for them.

And a war was what happened. People still talk about Tony Browne and Colin Lynch pulling on each other when the ball was thrown in at the start of that match, and no wonder, given the trouble it sparked for the rest of the summer in terms of suspensions and so on.

I had my hands full. Our information that we were in for a physical day was confirmed when I trotted up to mark Daly. The first thing that happened was, he welcomed me by hitting me a dig. I hit him back, and he hit me again. Between one thing and another I shoved him and that planted him on his arse. I wasn't a hard man or anything, but I had to stand up for myself; you have to win the battle first before you can play, and that goes for a lot of sports. I looked around for back-up when he hit me first and nobody was coming because they were all too busy with their own fights.

For instance, I looked across at Tony Browne and Colin Lynch flaking and in my view Lynch was way over the top. It was some pulling: they were giving out in Clare that he was suspended. If he did it now, the way discipline has gone in the GAA, I reckon he could get three or six months' suspension. He was a great hurler for Clare for years, and I wouldn't like to see any fella get a bad suspension, but I think he deserved the suspension he got that day. And when he was suspended, Ger Loughnane was talking about human rights!

It was going on all over the place. Greener and Jamesie were scrapping in the backs. Brian Lohan and Micheál White had a row further back on the field and both got sent off. Ollie Baker came swinging for our midfielder, Peter Queally, who was the right man for him because he swung back, so you had two gardaí, flaking away at each other in midfield.

It went on all over the field and Clare went to town on us. They bullied us physically – not so much beating us up as pushing us around. Hurling-wise, it was a wet day and we couldn't get our forwards going, and Clare were too strong and too experienced. They beat us well.

Unbelievable as it was to be in a Munster final, we ended up with nothing, and on top of that, Gerald and one of the selectors got a sideline suspension for the next outing in the championship for encroaching on the field, which meant a bad day had a nasty sting for us.

In time I got to know many of the Clare players. In 2005 on the All-Stars trip in Singapore, I got talking to Seanie McMahon and Brian Lohan one night, two lads I didn't know much about, but we had a few games of pool and after a few drinks we got on great. They beat myself and Dave Bennett and we had to pay up.

I didn't have many dealings with Seanie on the field but I came across Brian a few times. People talk about presence on the field: Lohan would be walking back and forth in front of the square and roaring out at you before the game started: 'You won't be coming in here today.' Whether he was trying to intimidate or frighten the opposition I don't know, but sometimes it worked for him and the opposition decided to take the option of a point rather than chancing a run down the centre.

The consolation for losing to Clare was playing in Croke Park against Galway in the All-Ireland quarter-final.

I'd been there in the mini-sevens, but most of our team

had never played a game there so it was a huge deal for us. In the GAA it's everybody's dream to play in Croke Park. The trouble is, nobody thinks about what the first time is like, and how tricky that might be. Our inexperience might have gone against us, but it was a help that the games were coming so fast: we didn't have time to dwell on the loss to Clare because we were out against Galway a week later. Little things that might have knocked us out of our stride completely if we'd been playing only once every four weeks took nothing out of us.

For example, we went to the wrong gate in Croke Park. The team bus had to reverse out and go all the way around the stadium to the right entrance, through the crowds, with supporters obviously wondering what we were doing backing a bus across the streets of Drumcondra. Nowadays that would be a complete disaster for our preparations – we'd nearly be thinking of it at half-time in the match, because everything is on a timetable up to the throw-in – but the funny thing was that it didn't take much out of us. We were going from big game to big game, and we were focused on the games, not the occasion.

Galway obviously thought they only had to turn up to beat us, but they didn't reckon on a couple of things we had going for us.

First, it was a huge emotional boost for us, as Waterford players, to run out in Croke Park for a championship game. And for our supporters. They were there in their thousands to see Waterford in Croke Park after over thirty-five years without a championship game there. We didn't want to let them down.

Tony Browne provided us with another boost. Everybody had been talking about him after the Munster final, saying there was no way he'd be playing against Galway that Sunday, that he wouldn't be up to it after the punishment he'd got, that he couldn't be right. But he went out that day and hurled every Galwayman who came near him up a stick. He was outstanding, but that's Tony Browne for you.

Tony's been playing for Waterford for seventeen years; put another way, he started playing inter-county hurling when Noel Connors was two years old, and now they're team-mates. He's a phenomenal man. He's in better shape now than he ever was. In 2010 Tony, Mullane, myself and a few others were given a different training programme early in the year, and Eoin Kelly met up with us one evening in the gym.

Eoin's a fit lad, but when Tony peeled off his top in the dressing room he nearly keeled over – Tony was built like Brad Pitt. He's not a drinker – he'd have the odd bottle, but that's it. You couldn't be a drinker and be built like that.

It was a great misfortune in 1998, when Tony won Hurler of the Year, that there wasn't as much recognition as there is now, with the Opel sponsorship of the GPA and so on. If he'd won it three or four years later, he'd have got more out of it.

Tony's a very, very smart man. Very deep. People don't know that about him because he doesn't put himself forward that much, but he's a pillar of the team.

The rest of us were mentally tougher than Galway after the season we'd had. We had to be. You can't beat hard championship matches and we'd played Tipperary, Clare twice, and we'd also had a tough league final against Cork. We were used to hitting the pace of a tough championship game as soon as the ball was thrown in because we'd been through it so often.

No team would have beaten us that day, not the way we were in the dressing room beforehand. Galway might have been many people's favourites, but the reality was they didn't stand a chance. We were well tuned in. We were ready.

By the time they got to grips with the game we'd won it and were in an All-Ireland semi-final. We celebrated well coming home on the bus with a few cans and a sing-song.

The big disappointment that year – bigger than losing the Munster final, even – was that it was our best chance of winning an All-Ireland. I'm convinced of that. I've often heard lads talking about having to lose an All-Ireland to win one, which sounds like rubbish to me. The proof of that is '98.

We had Kilkenny in the semi-final and it was a poor Kilkenny team by their standards. DJ Carey, Willie O'Connor and Pat O'Neill were all playing, but as a team they weren't the best Kilkenny ever put out. If they were being honest in Kilkenny they'd say so, particularly when you look at the quality of the team they put out against us ten years later in the 2008 All-Ireland final. The later team was the best ever to play the game; the earlier edition weren't world-beaters.

If we'd beaten them we'd have had no fear of Offaly in the All-Ireland final. We had lads who'd beaten them in an All-Ireland under-21 final in 1992. Having beaten Offaly in one All-Ireland, those players wouldn't have been intimidated facing them in another.

But we didn't get to the final. Kilkenny beat us in the semi-final with a fluky goal. DJ mishit a free and when it came across the field Niall Moloney pulled on the ball and scored a goal. Brian Flannery nearly got to him, but Moloney had the contact on the ball. A matter of a split-second, and the modern history of Waterford hurling could have been very different. When your luck is in, your luck is in. And when it's not . . .

At the other end Sean Daly had a great chance of a goal for us. The ball came across the square and Daly was close enough to kick it over the line, but he took a swing and Liam Keoghan hooked him. Ball cleared. Chance gone.

I got a couple of points off Liam Keoghan, but it was a disappointing day. We took the wrong options, we had bad wides, we were sending the ball in all wrong to the inside line . . . We had all the play and we just didn't take our chances.

Inexperience didn't help us. A lot of the Kilkenny lads had played plenty of times in Croke Park, and they were used to the surroundings – but being familiar with the way the grass grows on a field doesn't win a match for anyone. When they got chances, they took them. Simple as that.

It was hard for me watching the All-Ireland final that year, knowing I could have been there. On the bright side, I'd played a full season at inter-county level and done fairly well. I was nominated for an All-Star, but Michael Duignan of Offaly got the number ten jersey – though he could have been sent off in one of the games they played against Clare for a loose pull on an opponent, as I'm sure he remembers.

The All-Stars banquet was a highlight, travelling up to the Burlington Hotel with the other Waterford lads and seeing Tony win Hurler of the Year. We had a good night of it, and a good couple of days afterwards.

At the end of 1998 Colette became pregnant. I remember when we told her mother, the look she gave me . . . She wasn't impressed, to say the least – but my big fear was what Colette's father would say. Or do. I wondered if he'd give me a box. I needn't have worried – he was very good about it: he congratulated me and said we were old enough to make our own decisions.

Of course, then I had to go up and tell my mother, and if telling Colette's parents was nerve-racking, telling my own was absolutely terrifying. I left Colette in Dungarvan for that journey.

My mother didn't take the news very well at all, and the whole scene got a bit awkward, so after about twenty minutes of embarrassment and me hanging my head, I headed down to tell my grandmother. 'Don't worry about your mother,' she said. 'She'll get over it.'

I was coming away from my grandmother's house when I ran into my father at the foot of the hill. He gave me a look that would have cut three fellas in half.

But my grandmother was right, as she always was. After a few days they got used to the idea and started looking forward to the new arrival.

7

In 1998 there was one more change in my life. I got a tattoo. Tattoos suit some people and not others – they suit David Beckham, for instance, not that I'd be copying him in anything. But I'm interested in them. I watch that TV show *Miami Ink* about a tattoo parlour in the US.

Myself and the Chicken decided we'd get a couple done. We headed to Fermoy with Colette to this tattoo artist. He said he could do it that day so I got two small ones, a Celtic design on the arm and a cross. The discomfort didn't bother me but the Chicken never went back for another, so I'd say he didn't enjoy that aspect of it.

When my daughter Chloe was born I got her name tattooed on my forearm, and I got the original two changed to one big Celtic cross.

People probably zero in on the quote I have on my arm: 'If you don't know me, don't judge me.' That comes from a Colombian soccer player – in the 2002 World Cup I saw one of their games on TV and when a player got a goal he ran over to the camera and showed it off.

I felt it was true: what entitles anybody to judge another

person unless they know them? I headed to a tattoo artist in Waterford at Yakuza Tattoo and asked Dan if he could do it, and he offered me 'Only God can judge me', as an alternative. I insisted on my original choice, and he did a great job for me.

I try to follow that advice, and not judge people even though it's something we all do and I'm no exception. What I'd hope is that if someone sees my tattoo they take the lesson on board and don't make assumptions about people as readily as maybe they did before.

I've taken a lot of abuse from so-called hurling people and supporters – up to 2004 anyway: that year changed things for me – getting roared at by people on the terraces and in the stands – people judging me, in other words. Spectators who pay their money to go to matches are entitled to their opinions, but nobody's entitled to abuse players.

The lads sometimes asked about the tattoos, and where I'd got them, but like anything else, they became part of the furniture soon enough. Eoin Kelly has copied me all right, but he has a few to go to catch up. Eoin McGrath has some, so has Mullane – a good few lads have them in every county, but you wouldn't notice them. No opponent has ever mentioned them to me, or slagged me about them. Even compared to 1998, it's a common part of the culture now.

You have to go through a bit of pain for it. It takes a couple of hours while they use the needle to do the outline before they colour it in, but you get used to it.

The tattoos were part of the argument people were making a few years ago about Waterford being different – the celebrations on the pitch and all that – but that kind of discussion just becomes background noise, a buzz that you're not really aware of. The media are always looking for some kind of angle, something different, and that was part of it.

The tattoos aren't always well thought through. We were on a team holiday a few years ago in New York, and myself, Ken, Eoin McGrath and Jack Kennedy went on the lash, starting off near Ground Zero in the daytime and pushing through into the night. One of the lads wanted to go back to the hotel, so I helped him get a taxi but I couldn't get back into the nightclub the rest of them were in.

There I was, about to start wandering the streets of Manhattan, when I saw a tattoo parlour over the road. I headed in and got rosary beads with Chloe and Colette's names done on my back, but I was falling asleep while the tattooist was doing it.

The following morning I had one of those *What did I do last night?* moments. I wasn't long finding out when I had a shower.

That was all in the future, though. For us 1999 was full of promise. We were ready to build on 1998. Ready for progress.

Gerald had an announcement to make early on in 1999. There were rumours going around about Jimmy Barry-Murphy, who was managing the Cork hurlers: that he'd be stepping down before the Munster championship even began. He'd been in charge of Cork for three years and they didn't seem to be going anywhere, and the talk was that the Cork County Board had a shortlist of candidates to take over from him. The talk also had it that one of the people on the list was Gerald – naturally enough, given his record.

He cleared the air in the dressing room before training one evening in spring 1999. He said he wouldn't be heading back to take over the Cork team: he was committed to Waterford, and he'd never train another team against Waterford. (Of course, that speech backfired in 2007 when he managed Cork against us and we beat them twice in three championship games.)

In 1999 I'm not sure whether we felt there was much chance of him going back to Cork, but by committing to us he certainly drew the team together before we played in the championship.

I had my own worries. In January that year I broke my thumb in a challenge game against Limerick. I stuck my hand up for the ball and got a fair smack and knew immediately the thumb was broken.

I was out for four weeks, then went down to play Kilkenny and during the game I went up to bat the ball: smack. Broke the other thumb; sidelined for another four weeks.

That was tough enough, but there was no sparing me with the training: I still had to do all the running even though I had the thumbs in casts. The comments were predictable: 'Nobody runs on their hands, Dan. Away with you around the field.'

The training was good in 1999. We wanted to push on from 1998, to push on from reaching a Munster final and do better. We were meeting Cork in the championship – the Cork team that was going nowhere under Jimmy Barry-Murphy, supposedly. Given the talk that we'd heard, that

Jimmy was on the verge of leaving the Cork job only a few weeks before the championship, how well organized could they be?

We weren't afraid of Cork. We'd played them in the league final the previous year, which had been close, but we were missing Seanie Cullinane that day, and though Mark O'Sullivan did well for us at full-back, he was caught under one high ball and Seanie O'Farrell buried a goal for Cork – the goal that won them the league title. We'd lost narrowly. But we'd be at full strength for the game in the Munster championship.

So we weren't intimidated. The one thing about a Cork team was that we'd be able to hurl against them rather than have to take on a physical battle. Other teams might be more physical but we could always play the game against Cork, and we were confident we had better players than them. Then, ahead of the championship game, they named their team and had six debutants down to play against us, inexperienced youngsters, and five of them were under-21s.

By contrast, we'd beaten Tipperary the previous year and drawn against Clare in the Munster final. We wouldn't have thought we were top of the heap, but we felt we were further along as a team than the Cork side we were up against – older and tougher.

The thing is, though, new players can play with freedom because they have no fear. Cork's new players did well for them – I was marking one of the debutants, Wayne Sherlock, who was an outstanding hurler, and I got three points. Flynn and Ken were outstanding that day as well, but we lost one huge battle.

The big advantage for Cork was that Mickey O'Connell destroyed Tony Browne in the middle of the field, scoring nine points from frees and play. Mickey was an outstanding hurler who'd give anyone a tough hour, but Tony had injured his ankle in training a couple of weeks before the game, and he came back playing too soon. He should have given the ankle time to rest and recover, but we were playing a Munster championship game. He was always going to line out.

O'Connell picked up the Man of the Match award that day, and he deserved it, but Tony wasn't right. There would have been pressure on Tony anyway as the current Hurler of the Year, but he wasn't fit so he didn't have a chance. As it turned out, he took a year afterwards to get over that injury fully.

Unfortunately for us, the bad news didn't end there. Fergal Hartley was playing midfield with Tony, and in one of the first clashes of the game he broke a finger. So we had one midfielder who could barely run and another who could barely hold the hurley.

Cork beat us by four points. Another summer gone. And Jimmy Barry-Murphy not only stayed on but brought Cork to the All-Ireland. So much for a Cork team that was going nowhere.

When I was growing up in Lismore Cork were the big neighbours that you'd hear about all the time, the team that would put manners on you. To this day, despite the fact that we've beaten them more often in the last ten or twelve years than they've beaten us, if Cork were playing Waterford in tiddlywinks they'd think they could beat us. They have something about them – call it tradition, call it arrogance, call it what you like – and no matter what Waterford team they're up against, they feel they'll be able to beat us.

Even before the 2010 Munster final, which was about as fifty–fifty a game as you could imagine (proved by the fact that there were only three points between us after 160 minutes), the word came over from Cork: they were full sure they'd beat us.

We had first come across each other at senior level in 1998, when they beat us in the National League final, but as the years went on, the rivalry between the two groups of players grew stronger and stronger. There was a bit of background to it. They'd embarrassed us in two Munster minor finals in Thurles in 1994 and 1995 – well, 'embarrassed' is one way to put it: 'hammered the shit out of us' would be a better description.

If anyone had seen those games they'd have picked out Seán Óg and Dónal Óg and the other lads playing for Cork as the men who'd go on and make it, but we licked our wounds and then went back to it. We got down to work and we improved. We matured and got physically stronger, and most important of all, we got cuter.

After the loss against Cork in 1999, there was huge disappointment. We'd put in the same amount of work as we had in 1998 and felt we'd make another Munster final at least. We ended up with nothing.

Over-confidence? Maybe that was a factor; some of us probably took our eye off the ball and felt we'd be able to handle a team with six debutants. We were wrong – though in hindsight, some of those debutants were lads like Sherlock, Timmy McCarthy, Ben O'Connor and Dónal Óg Cusack. Not a bad assortment.

People forget, too, that even though it was only a few years ago, there was no back door, apart from the provincial finalists, and all our work was gone after seventy minutes. That was wrong. The back door was a great idea in that regard, and people who say there are too many games now are way off the mark: you can never have too many games. It was one of the better ideas the GAA had. The challenges various teams faced in keeping themselves fresh when there were a few weeks between games – ourselves included – were just a by-product of the new system, which everybody had to get used to.

The same is true for teams facing the opposite problem, too many games coming too fast: we all learned when the back door was introduced that one draw, one replay, could lead to a team playing three games in three weeks, with disastrous consequences. But that was all in the future.

We were probably a little unlucky, too, that the 'full' back door, if you like – the second chance for teams that lost a first-round game – didn't come in for a year or two after that. I think we'd have developed a little more quickly with more championship games. We'd have learned where to play certain lads, what approach would suit us in certain games, but it wasn't to be.

What was depressing altogether was that Cork went on to win the All-Ireland. We knew we weren't far off it, which didn't make the summer any better.

8

On 19 June 1999, at quarter to nine, my daughter Chloe was born. It was the proudest day of my life. Any reader who is a father knows that feeling. It changes your life.

She was six weeks premature, and though I wasn't a parenting expert, I could tell that wasn't good news. I wasn't allowed in for the delivery because she was so premature, but having the doctor come out and say, 'You have a baby daughter,' was fantastic.

When she was born she had to go into an incubator, and obviously we were worried. You make a lot of deals in your mind when you see a helpless, tiny baby in a glass compartment and you're not able to do anything. You start thinking, *If she comes through I'll do this or that; if she's okay I'll do anything I have to do.* The frustration is something alive in you and even the normal worries you had before the baby was born seem like the happiest times of your life in comparison.

She got through, though, and we didn't care about anything once she was healthy. Neither did my parents, of course.

At the time we were living in Bridget's Terrace in

Dungarvan and it was freezing: that's my abiding memory of that time. We had all the usual stuff – 'It's your turn to feed the child'; 'I have to get up for work in the morning, you can stay in bed' – but it was amazing. There's nothing like sitting down, holding your baby in your arms and feeding her.

Chloe is the best girl in the world; she's Daddy's girl and if anybody were to say anything about her, well, God help them. She's the greatest thing ever to come into my life. When she's buzzing around the house it's a brighter place, and if I'm nervous coming up to a big game, the two of us usually head out shopping to Dungarvan. The craic we have together relaxes me totally.

Once she was at a game when some moron sitting near her was roaring abuse at me, as she told me later. I was about to say to her not to mind fools like that, but she piped up, 'It's okay, I stuck up for you, Daddy.'

What could I say to that?

After Chloe arrived it was another responsibility, and I just got on with it. The way I was brought up, if you wanted something your parents would do their best to get it for you, and I'm the same with Chloe.

The funny thing was that the lads on the team were delighted for me. There wouldn't have been many fathers among them at that time. And I'd never blame her for loss of form or anything like that, but when you have a child, hurling goes out the door for a while. Everything does. You mightn't be able to put the effort into training or whatever, and you can see it affecting a player for a while, until the child gets a bit bigger. It affects everything, the night feeds and changing nappies and so on. All of that is a big change, a big adjustment.

One time when Chloe was two or three she was unwell and I brought her up to the hospital in Ardkeen. The doctor gave her an injection for the infection she had and she was roaring. She looked up into my eyes, as if to say, 'Daddy, make him stop.' It was the worst experience of my life – I was crying myself – and you wouldn't have much mind for hurling after that.

Thanks to Donal I'd changed jobs by then, too. Coming into 1998, I got a job with Waterford Crystal in Dungarvan, luckily enough, and I was put into the semi-skilled area, burning toxic acids, looking for chips off the glass and so on, with the great Pat Hickey. He was a tough man at his job and demanded you worked properly, which was only right. I made great friends there in Watty, Pat Fitz, Big John Power, Gerry Boland, the Riordans and Crotty brothers, Joe Power and Joe Hallahan. We had great banter and they were good with the work, though it was hard enough going in at eleven, working until six and then heading off to training before going back to work until twelve.

At times you'd have to beg lads to let you off, which nobody would enjoy – it was as if they had something over you – but when I was working with great people it was much better. I'd work away on my own, the headphones on, 2FM or WLR blasting away, polishing glass. Or sometimes I'd slip into the jacks for a nap if I had a bit of a head.

A machine was brought in to do the job and three of us were put on three shifts for it – I'd be on nights, which I enjoyed, keeping an eye on the computer. That was fair enough, but the changes weren't all for the better.

I know that some readers will probably shake their heads when they read what I've said about Tony and Fergal being injured against Cork in '99. They might think I'm making excuses, complaining about the breaks of the game. But the breaks can have a huge influence on a game, or a season, or a career. The year after we'd played with two crocked midfielders, we were well on the way to a win in the Munster championship that would have opened up the year for us when a freak injury sent us off the rails.

Ken McGrath's injury is my strongest memory of 2000. We were playing Tipperary in the Munster championship quarter-final down in Páirc Uí Chaoimh – or, rather, Ken was playing, and beating, Tipperary on his own. He was giving an exhibition – with very little help from the rest of us – but it didn't last until half-time.

He was coming across the field with the ball and he just went down as though he'd been shot. We knew immediately it was bad – Ken just doesn't go down. He's an awesome player, an awesome man.

At half-time we could see that his leg was destroyed; it was swollen and discoloured, but he was too valuable to take off. He got a few injections in the leg, but it was too bad an injury and eventually he had to be substituted. I've no doubt we'd have beaten them if Ken hadn't been injured. He was marking Philly Maher, who was a good full-back, but Ken had him in his pocket that day.

Since 1998 Ken has been the most consistent player

Above: My father, Brian (*centre*), played for Waterford in his day.

Left: Daniel Shanahan: my grandfather.

Left: Hurling was my favourite subject in school! (*Left to right*): Brendan Landers, Thomas Landers, Dave Bennett and myself.

Below: A big day: playing in Croke Park at the age of twelve, before the Offaly–Antrim All-Ireland semi-final in 1989.

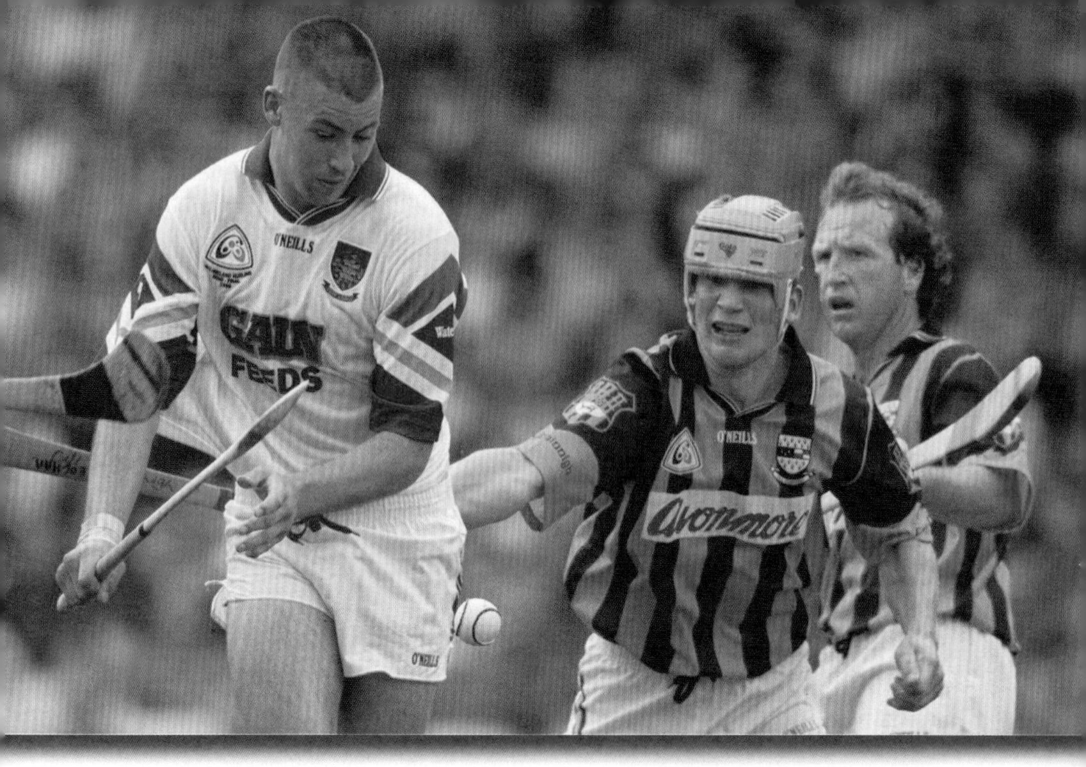

Above: The 1998 All-Ireland semi-final v. Kilkenny. Was it our best chance to capture the big one? Myself with Liam Keoghan and Willie O'Connor.

Below: Munster final replay 'battle', 1998: (*left to right*) Sean McMahon, Ken McGrath, myself, Anthony Daly, Tony Browne and Colin Lynch.

Above: Tussling with Davy Fitzgerald, in goal for Clare in the 2004 Championship. I put three balls in Davy's net that day.

Below: Celebrating after scoring against Tipperary in the 2004 Munster semi-final.

Claiming the *sliotar* from Cork's John Gardiner on the way to our 2004 Munster final victory.

Above: Catching my breath with Cork's Diarmuid 'Sully' O'Sullivan in a National Hurling League match in 2007 – 'I'm fucked, Sully'; 'If you're fucked, I'm fucked myself, Dan.'

Below: Having words with Seán Óg Ó hAilpín during the same match.

Waterford has had. I couldn't speak highly enough of the man: we're good friends and we've been on the same team from underage up, which means we've known each other about twenty years. (Of course, that doesn't mean he'd spare me any more than anyone else. I marked him in an under-21 county final one time and he broke a hurley off my elbow: halved me. That's Ken. He has no problem letting you have it. And he had good reason to that day: I got 1–3 off him and he had to be moved away from me at half-time. The referee that day was Paul Kelly, who became a hurley-carrier with Waterford afterwards, incidentally.)

When Ken was taken off that day in Cork, you could see the heads going down. The confidence drains out of a team when a player who's giving a performance like that has to go off with an injury. But that also shows what experience means. To most followers 'experience' probably translates as 'player in his early thirties', but if you jumped forward four years from the day Ken was injured, we played the same team in the same stadium in the Munster championship. We lost Tony Browne before the start of the 2004 Munster semi-final against Tipp, while Paul Flynn and Ken were both taken off before the end. If a neutral observer had been told that those three players wouldn't be on the field at the final whistle, he'd probably have put his mortgage on Tipperary; yet we won that game.

It was defeats like that Munster quarter-final in 2000 that taught us the lesson. We knew to keep going to the very end, because one goal, one break, one slip could make the difference.

We'd have needed more than one break in 2000, however.

panel, if you don't have competition for places you can get complacent, and we were probably slipping.

Nowadays in Waterford there's real competition. There might be one or two lads whose positions are safe, but nobody else can sit back and say, 'Well, he'll have to pick me.' That makes us sharper in training, and makes the lads we mark in training sharper, which all feeds into creating a more professional squad.

It was different around 1999 and 2000. That competition didn't exist, even though other teams were taking us more seriously. It was nobody's fault, just a case of improving standards in the entire county and having better underage structures and coaching. That led eventually to competition in the panel, but in 2000 it was all in the future. Put another way, the lads who were contributing to the competition on the panel in 2010 were children of ten or eleven in 2000.

It might be a contradiction, then, to say that at the same time I was under a bit of pressure. It was my third year on the panel and because I was a regular I was regarded differently.

Things change when you're an established player on the team because people have expectations. Whether that's good or bad is a matter for debate. Sometimes I get a kick out of, say, the television build-up to a big game, when you see head shots of players on-screen as the commentators go through what each one is like and his form that season. To me that level of scrutiny is well over the top. You see the same thing ahead of a Heineken Cup or Six Nations game, where a player's form is put under the microscope – but for those players, playing their sport is also their full-time job.

The pressure shows in different ways – not from the selectors but from other teams and other players, who would have seen what I was like as a player and would have had the opportunity to study how I played, for instance. Opposing managers would know I was good under the high ball because they'd seen me play a few times. As a result they'd get their defenders to break the ball away from me rather than contesting it and trying to catch it alongside me.

An inter-county player has a couple of years before the opposition catches on to his game. Then you have to adapt or you're sunk: the hurling world is small so if it gets around that you don't like to get the ball high then you can be sure that that's the only way the opposition will allow it in to you.

The other downer about that year was hearing commentators and pundits, not to mind the public, saying, 'Oh, Waterford are finished now.' I've been hearing that from people every year since I started back in 1996. Every year the papers say it, or the pundits on television say it – 'Last year was Waterford's year. They're gone past it now because the team that made the breakthrough for them in 1998 is just too old to keep going.' What nobody's noticed is that, over the years, Gerald and Justin McCarthy and Davy Fitzgerald have brought in new players – no big clear-outs, just one or two new lads every year.

People fixate on Tony Browne, because he started off back in 1992, and get it into their heads that the whole team is that age, when everybody knows that no one in the country is as old as Tony (sorry about that, kid). I suppose it's just an easy label to throw on a team – 'They're gone past it.' They'll have to be right one of the years if they keep saying it.

9

It was no surprise that 2001 finished Gerald. It nearly finished a lot of us.

Given that we were a bit stale in 2000, we had good newcomers the next year. Seamus Prendergast, a big, powerful man, was a good addition to the panel – though he'd been on the fringes in 1999 – and took a lot of pressure off other lads. He was a great fella to have alongside you in the trenches. Seamus's strength was a big asset to us in the half-forward line, as he kept opposition defenders on the back foot physically.

Then we had John Mullane. There's a lad who has realized his potential. He always had the speed, and at that time he could be easily spotted in his red helmet, flying around the place for De La Salle, but nobody could have guessed he'd turn out to be as good as he's become. That's down to his own hard work: Mullane has improved his touch and his shooting through long, lonely hours of training, nothing else. People see the bright sunshine of a championship day but they don't realize that the tools you use that afternoon are a long time being prepared on winter evenings.

We were cruising in Páirc Uí Chaoimh, 2–5 to 0–1 up against Limerick after fifteen minutes. Absolutely cruising. Everything we touched turned into a goal or a point. It was one of those dream days that a team gets. Seamus was well involved; Mullane was running riot that day as well.

Then it started going wrong. Mullane got injured off the ball and was substituted, and Limerick started coming back into it. Seanie Cullinane was caught under a high ball and Brian Begley got a goal. When they got the momentum, it was hard to get a foothold against it, and we just got sucked in. We weren't cute enough that day, clearly. In my view, we should have got one of them down with a hamstring or something to break up their momentum.

Anyone who's ever played the game will tell you that at certain times in a match the opposition hit a period when they're on top: the clearances they launch upfield without looking go straight to teammates; the over-the-shoulder shots from out on the wing drop over the bar; the defenders win a ball over the heads of opponents and then win a free when they drive out.

When that happens you have two options: you can play them on their terms or you can play them on your terms. If you take the latter option one of your teammates gets a sudden cramp and the doctor has to come out to see what's wrong. Then you ask the referee if he's seen what the full-back is doing, and the full-back get thick and starts arguing with you, and the referee is telling you to buzz off because he wants the doctor off the field and the game to restart, and the opposition is getting thick because they know what you're doing. Then one of your teammates wins the next ball and the other crowd have lost the momentum. You've got it.

We probably still aren't cute enough that way. You see other teams do it: a player goes down for a breather when their opponents are dominating the play. You see them do it against you and it's frustrating, but it's our own fault that we don't do it ourselves.

The loss to Limerick destroyed us. And it ended Gerald as Waterford manager. He had said to us himself that he'd know when to go as manager, which might have been a hard thing to say. While I don't think he said in the dressing room afterwards that he was going, we knew.

In five years we hadn't won a trophy, but I think Gerald was unlucky. He laid the foundations and he brought in the discipline. That wasn't always easily done, either.

Back in 1998, we were training in Walsh Park – a desperate night, rain and mud – and Brian Greene wasn't in good form after he'd been taken off in a match the week before. We had a meeting after training, and when Gerald stood up to speak, Greener said, 'I have something to say.' Gerald responded: 'I'm talking.' So they ended up going into the next room together.

I was sitting right next to the dressing-room door and I could hear the shouting going on between them. We all could.

Then Gerald came in, said, 'I'm off.' He took his bag and went home.

There was talk of some Mount Sion lads dropping off the panel to back Greener, but in the end they didn't go against Gerald. There were clear-the-air talks eventually, which sorted things out between Gerald and Greener, which was no harm.

I was just happy I wasn't marking Greener that evening in training.

Gerald was a good coach and a good manager – they're two different jobs. A coach improves your hurling, your touch, your shooting; a manager keeps the team positive and motivated. It's not everybody who can do both.

The one thing we were missing under Gerald was consistency. That was always lacking. No matter who we played against, they thought they had a chance against Waterford. They all reckoned it depended on which Waterford turned up: if the good Waterford turned up, scoring goals for fun, nobody could live with us, but if the bad Waterford turned up, leaking scores, they knew they had a chance.

We discussed that, and would try to put it to bed, but we couldn't. The likes of Hartley, Frampton, Cullinane would say in the dressing room, 'Let's put this inconsistency thing to bed. Let's earn the respect.' Yet to this day it's an issue – no matter who we play, they feel they have a chance.

9 March 2010: Semple Stadium, Tipperary v Waterford, National Hurling League

Thurles again. The Square, the bus journey up over that hump-backed bridge. A familiar trip to us at this stage.

I'm starting today on Padraic Maher. A serious, serious player. He gave some exhibition against Kilkenny in the All-Ireland final last year for a young fella of twenty. I'm looking forward to it, though. It's my first league game of the year against one of the top players in the game. It's a challenge. After months of sweating in the gym, this is the pay-off. We shake hands before the throw-in with him. Quiet. A few full-backs would be into your ear straight away – one of the men who wore that jersey before him, Philly Maher, often had a good bit to say for himself – but this lad says nothing.

Within a couple of minutes I knew I had his number that day. The first ball I get, I turn to take him on, and he's standing off me, giving me a yard or two: that tells me he's afraid I'm too fast for him, that he doesn't want to chance playing the ball from the front for fear I'll get him on the turn and he won't be able to recover to catch me.

I fade away from him and go for a point, and the umpire

bends for the flag. There's only a few thousand here but the score gets a good reaction from the Waterford supporters who've travelled.

The game is decent. Tipp take a five-point lead but we reel them in. Our Eoin Kelly punishes them from frees. I rustle up two points myself, though Maher wins a fair few balls as well. He's a Thurles Sarsfields man, and there's a fair roar when he comes out with the ball; they don't shout too much when I get a pass away to Stephen Molumphy for a goal for us.

With time running out we're a point down, but we manage one last attack. I come on to a ball out on the 21 and collect it. I step inside Maher and he grabs me: free. He complains to the referee, Cathal McAllister, and he's right to complain. It's a soft one. If it was a Munster final the ref wouldn't have blown.

Eoin bangs it over and it's a draw. When the final whistle goes I'm penned in by reporters down in the corner by the Killinan End.

'You're back, Dan,' they say. 'You must be happy.'

I am. I'd say I was never gone.

10

The year Justin McCarthy got the job as Waterford hurling manager, 2002, I was on steroids. There's no need to call the Irish Sports Council drug testers just yet. I wasn't looking to increase my biceps size, nor to mind enhance my performance on the hurling field.

Early on in the year I'd been having trouble with my knees and ankles: they were very sore and at times I could barely walk. Once or twice it was an ordeal to get out of the car, let alone go training. I went to see our team doctor, Tom Higgins, a great man, and he took my bloods and eventually came up with a diagnosis for me: I had polyarthritis.

I couldn't believe it – it was a desperate blow to me in terms of my general health, never mind my hurling career – but he was optimistic, saying he hoped it'd be temporary. He was going to put me on steroids to help clear it up. We wrote to Croke Park to make sure we weren't breaking any rules, and once it was cleared with the authorities I started the drug.

I could feel the effects immediately. In pictures from that season, you can see I'm blown up, swollen by the drug compared to previous years. Bloated. Nobody asked why I looked so different, but then again, I was on the fringes of the team. Bit-part players don't get many questions; people only want to hear opinions from the first fifteen.

To go back to the beginning of the Justin regime, I had some inkling about him before he ever came in to take Waterford over, a move which involved Paddy Joe Ryan of the county board. Justin was in charge of a club team in Cork who played against Lismore. Dave Bennett was missing for us that day, so I got put on the frees, and my eye was in: I got six or seven. That was my first encounter with Justin McCarthy, him watching me fire over half a dozen frees from all angles. A good impression, you'd think.

At that stage I didn't know he'd be Waterford manager, obviously. I'd heard he was a fine player in his day and read his column in the *Examiner* the odd time. Clearly he knew the game inside out, but I wouldn't have known much about his background as a player or coach.

On the panel we'd assumed the county board would go 'outside' for a manager, though Jim Greene from Mount Sion was interested in replacing Gerald, but Justin's appointment was a bit of a surprise. He'd been out of inter-county coaching for a good few years. On closer inspection his CV was good, but it still required that close inspection: he'd coached Cork, Clare and Antrim in the seventies and eighties, but that's the dim and distant past to the modern player. He'd been involved with Cashel King Cormacs when they'd won the Tipp county title and the Munster club championship, but even that had been a good ten years before he came to Waterford, and there weren't many lads left playing from that time who could give him a reference.

Our first impressions of him were good, though. We met him as a panel in Davitts in Dungarvan, and he did all the talking. Literally. He talked about where Waterford hurling was going, and about where he wanted to bring us. He also introduced Seamie Hannon and Colm Bonnar, who were coming in as selectors with him, but he stressed that he'd be doing all the hurling, all the coaching.

The minute he started speaking, you listened. He had that intensity about him – his way or no way. That was the distinct impression I got from him.

Gerald was different. You could sit down with Gerald and have a pint, chat about different sports – he was interested in golf and soccer, not just hurling. I'm not a player who'd kiss a manager's arse to keep on the team, or to get on it in the first place, but I enjoyed chatting away with Gerald and the craic we had together.

When we were on the team holiday in 1998, for example, we had a great time, and he was out dancing and boogieing the night away with the players – having the craic with us, and dying sick on the bus on the way to the airport.

Gerald could be one of the lads. He'd let the hair down the odd time and we'd have a good session with him. He wouldn't do it that often – a manager has to have a certain amount of distance from his players, and I think even players prefer it that way – but we could get away from the hurling with Gerald. He appreciated that we had lives outside of the game.

It wasn't like that with Justin. If you were talking to him, it was hurling, all hurling, all the time. Obviously that can get a bit intense and fellas can get sick of it, but we became sick of it a lot later in our relationship with Justin.

The first night we trained with Justin it was in Clashmore, because that was one of the few grounds in the county that had floodlights at that time. We were looking forward to it: people talked a lot about him as a coach, and they were right to talk. He was first class.

The first thing he would do was to look at each player's hurley and bring it away with him if he felt it wasn't good enough. He'd always be talking about how even good inter-county hurlers didn't know what size their hurley was, or how heavy, that they weren't getting the most out of it, and he was right.

He'd lighten the hurley, or trim it down, or work on the handle. Some of them were beyond help, he'd say; he might look at your hurley and say to you, 'That hurley's only good for signing autographs; it's no good for you.' A player might think he had a cracker of a hurley, or it might be one he'd got a few scores with in a big game, a lucky hurley, and Justin would be telling him it was fit for nothing.

On that first training session in Clashmore, a cold night, we didn't touch the ball. We were pulling on the grass, swinging away on fresh air – no ball – working on the speed of the pull. The aim of those drills was to work on the wrists, getting them stronger and more flexible, more used to what Justin needed. Another technique was to hold the hurley straight up in your hand and Justin would get you to flick it from side to side, working your wrists the whole time.

He had a load of drills like that, to improve our speed

with the hurley. Left and right, in the air and on the ground . . . A few lads were asking, 'What's going on here?' but it's not like they were questioning it. After a session the blood would be running down your arms from the blisters on your hand.

Of course, we knew well it was also a test. We had to get used to it and improve our speed with the hurley or we were gone.

Then, when Justin introduced the ball to sessions, we loved it. Because of what we'd been doing without the ball, our speed was good enough for when we were in the middle of a line, with fellas sending the ball into us from either side. We'd improved almost unknown to ourselves.

As I say, though, there were a few signs early on of Justin's attitude to players if you were cute enough to see them, particularly when it came to his pet subject: the hurley.

For instance, he wouldn't have paid much attention to my hurley in the early days because I wasn't really part of his plans. There was a very easy way for players on the Waterford panel to work out their importance in the scheme of things: they'd figure out whether they were part of Justin's plans or not, depending on how much attention he was paying to their hurleys.

Once in a while he'd look at my hurley, but it was only occasionally, compared to the lads who were on the starting fifteen, and I got the message soon enough. I didn't get too many starts and I soon began thinking, *Do I stick or fold?*

That was a serious question for me. I was twenty-five, physically mature, and had been a regular on the team from 1998 to 2001, contributing scores regularly from play against the top teams. Now the new manager didn't fancy me.

It wasn't as if I didn't have other interests. I could have done without the hassle of getting off work for training, and Colette would have appreciated the help with Chloe, who was as much of a handful as any healthy, inquisitive three-year-old would be.

I wasn't alone. Nowadays in inter-county hurling, teams carry a fair number of players in the squad, which is a help if you're a manager who wants to have fifteen-a-side games in training, but it isn't as helpful when you know that that's all you're there for – to fill out the B-team in the mixed match at the end of the training session.

I'd say to this day Justin would still have his seventeen to twenty players in his head, his starting fifteen with maybe a few first-choice substitutes, while the others on the panel are only there to tog out for matches at training and so on. At the time, in 2002, that was my job: making up the numbers in training.

Maybe I wasn't up to his speed of hurling; we all could tell that quick striking and a super first touch were what he wanted out of his players, but the frustrating thing was that I didn't know. I knew that I wasn't part of it because the selectors weren't talking to me, which seemed to me to be a total waste of time.

If the management feel you're good enough for the senior county panel but not good enough to start, then that's fair enough. That's the job of management in every sport: to make a call about their players. They live or die by those decisions.

But what are the rest of the players there for, if that's the case? Surely if you have a squad of players you should try to improve their skills in case you need to call on them as substitutes in a game. If the manager doesn't do that, the players will keep making the same mistakes and they won't progress. Then, when you have a couple of injuries or suspensions in the first fifteen and you look at your bench, you'll realize you've failed because you haven't improved those players enough. Or else you'll look at the bench and you'll see nothing at all, because those players will have figured out a long time beforehand that they're just filling out places in mixed matches, and they'll have packed it in.

Having said all that, Justin's training was good for players. It brought me on, certainly. I could see the improvement, and my touch was better. But sometimes that could be even more frustrating – I was a better player but I wasn't getting a start, and I wasn't being told what I could do differently in order to get one.

It wasn't a vicious circle. It was a vicious dead-end.

I think Justin had probably come down to Waterford with his first fifteen or seventeen already picked in his mind. He knew the club scene in Waterford well and he had his mind made up about players.

I wasn't the only one who felt frozen out, either. One night in Ballymacarbry we were training in one part of the field, the outfield players, while Justin trained Stevie Brenner, one of the 'keepers, in another. Brendan Landers, who had been first-choice goalkeeper under Gerald, was sent to train with us outfield players while Justin trained

Stevie. Landers is a Lismore man, and people might think I'm biased, but he'd been outstanding for us in 1998, a huge part of the run we'd had. He was a fantastic shot-stopper and had a great puck-out. A few of the backs might have said he gave out to them a lot, and maybe he wouldn't have been the most encouraging 'keeper to play in front of, but he got the job done for us.

That night in Ballymacarbry finished him. Goalkeeping is such a specialized position that you need extra coaching and different drills all the time. He was getting nothing done training with us outfield players. Even if he'd been sitting on his backside at the other end of the pitch, watching Justin give Stevie goalkeeping tips, it would have been of more benefit to him.

He's the kind of fella who wouldn't stick around just to carry the hurleys, and in the car on the way home he told me he'd had enough of it; he could tell Justin didn't rate him. It was a pity, because if he'd stayed around and bitten his tongue, he'd have made the 2004 Munster final team, and that year might have had a different ending for all of us if we'd had him in goal, but he didn't think he had a future with Justin.

I wouldn't blame him. When he packed it in not long afterwards, I was disappointed for him – and for us. I'm not being wise after the event about the next couple of seasons after Brendan left, but good 'keepers are hard to come by, as Justin found out.

I was finding out about life in the wilderness myself. Andy Moloney, Eoin McGrath and Micheál White were all starting ahead of me, when I felt I should have been on the team, but I kept the head down and kept working away.

That's discipline. People ask about discipline and what it means, and some think it's a matter of not getting yellow cards or provoked in big games, but there's more to it, and that's a good example. You have to keep going, keep working.

I found it hard to face training when I knew there wasn't much chance of starting, but I had confidence in myself that I could turn it around if I put in the effort. What's the point in crying off, anyway? I'd only be cutting my nose off to spite my face. My attitude is, you must be a man about it and train hard. What's the alternative? If you packed it in you'd be sitting at a bar counter boring lads with stories of how you played in a Munster final one time, and while you're boring them you'd be thinking, *What would have happened if I'd stayed on?*

But there were still nights when it was hard going, and hard to go. I'd sit in the car in Dungarvan, ready to head to Walsh Park, and think, *What the hell am I doing? Why am I wasting my time?* It was a toss-up some nights whether I'd turn the key in the ignition or not. I could have been with Chloe at home and giving Colette a break. It was hard on her that I was gone a couple of nights a week: it was a big commitment, and with nothing to show for it in the way of a starting place on the team.

11

For all the undoubted improvements that Justin brought to our skill levels, come the championship, we needed a bit of magic in Thurles to get us past Cork in the semi-final.

It was a wet, miserable, windy day with a small crowd, and there wasn't much between the teams all through the game. The slippery conditions influenced the result, certainly. We didn't have many clear-cut goal chances but Tony Browne raised a green flag. Dónal Óg Cusack let in a howler from Tony, a ball from miles out the field that shot off the grass past him. Of course, Dónal Óg is three times the 'keeper now to what he was back then. The goal was a gift that he would hardly repeat these days, but we were happy to put it in our pockets.

I came on as a substitute and did OK, but it was another substitute who made the difference. Ken McGrath had been injured for that game – he could hardly lift his arm above his shoulder – but Justin threw him on with a few minutes to go to see what he could do up front, and he won the game for us.

I can remember vividly the point he got to win it: the ball

was loose and Brian Greene came through from the middle of the field, won the ball, broke a tackle and popped it to Ken. He just took a snap shot and put it over the Cork bar at the Killinan End, toppling over backwards. Some achievement for a man who'd had problems getting his arm into the jersey when we were in the dressing room before the throw-in.

There was no great celebrating. The day was so wet and the crowd so small that it was as if we'd won a league game. Small potatoes stuff. The teams had played well in the conditions, and there was no more than a point between us the whole day, but we'd won, and it's hard to overstate how important the win was.

To me it was the victory that set everything in motion, and a lot of credit has to go to the man who came in to manage us that year. I couldn't say if it was luck or not, but having Justin McCarthy come in just as our rivalry with Cork was about to take off was a huge help. He'd played for Cork, he'd coached Cork and he knew the club scene well, so there was no aspect of Cork hurling that he couldn't go into detail about.

The one lesson he was trying to hammer home the whole time was that we were just as good as them. You might say that's fairly obvious now, but it wasn't when he started. After that win we were confident in ourselves – and in him as a manager. Which was just as well, given that Tipp were now red-hot favourites for the Munster title.

There had been some adjustments in the team. When Seanie Cullinane stepped down in 2001 – just before we won our Munster title, unfortunately – Tom Feeney stepped in to man the full-back slot. He was another strong character on the field. In one game, Ken McGrath happened to take Paul O'Brien out. In the same game, not long after, Tony happened to take Paul out again, and then we heard this roar from the full-back position: 'Would the pair of ye cop the fuck on?' It was Feeney.

Tom was one of the most intelligent players we had, without a doubt. He was my roommate on holidays and when we overnighted with the team. He was outstanding that way. He would always say the right thing at the right time on the morning of a match to put you at your ease.

Mind you, Tom got into difficulty off the field on one occasion. Our first holiday ever with the Waterford team, back in 1998, saw us heading out to the Canaries. There we were, a big gang of us, going mad for the sun and the pool the second we threw our bags into our hotel rooms. Down with us to the pool and in jumps Tom, straight into the deep end. He came up and shouted, 'Help,' and back down again he sank.

'Good man, Tom,' we shouted back, trying to figure out where the bar was.

Up he came again – 'Please, help me' – then down he sank.

We were wondering if he was for real when he came back up: 'PLEASE, PLEASE, HELP ME!' The physio, Shay Fitzpatrick, jumped in and pulled him out.

He was for real; the poor guy had jumped in the deep end by mistake and was on the verge of drowning; we thought he was pulling our legs. If it hadn't been for Shay Fitzpatrick, we'd have gone back to Waterford a man short.

*

I remember Babs Keating telling a newspaper in 2002 that Tipp would probably win the Munster title by ten points, and he wouldn't have been alone in thinking that all they had to do was turn up on the day. Maybe that favouritism affected them. Tipperary are a different kettle of fish from Cork.

Growing up in Lismore, I never had many dealings with Tipperary, but you'd hear plenty from the lads along the border – Waterford people up around Carrick-on-Suir – about the Tipperary attitude. It's hardly a surprise to hear that most people view Tipperary as fairly arrogant when it comes to hurling, and it's true that their followers can be a bit hard to take at times.

Not the players, of course – most of them I've always found pretty sound. Eoin Kelly of Mullinahone is as sound a guy as you could meet, and great craic on a night out, not to mention one of the most talented hurlers I've ever seen. Eamonn Corcoran is the same, a grand guy; he was as clean a player as you could meet.

I made the Railway Cup team in 1999 and after one game, myself and Peter Queally decide to shorten the journey in Gerry Chawke's, in Clonmel, for a few beers. We met up with Tommy Dunne there and we had a great night with him.

The likes of Babs Keating probably don't do the image of Tipperary many favours at times, I reckon. He's often quoted in the media and I'd wonder if the lads on the Tipp panel and management are that fond of seeing him pop up whenever they lose a game.

No matter who the Tipp manager is, though, the constant was the arrogance of the supporters, the sense that they were the real king-pins when it came to hurling, even though they'd only won one All-Ireland since the nineties.

It's because of that attitude that I'd prefer to have to lose to Cork any day of the week than to Tipp. Cork would hurl you and you'd have the banter with the supporters every time, but people viewed Tipp as arrogant. No doubt about it.

I saw it at first hand myself at the start of the late 90s, when there was a fundraising game put on down in Carrick-on-Suir, and we took on Tipperary. Until we rolled into the dressing rooms I had had no idea of the hatred that existed down there between the Tipp crowd on one side and the Waterford crowd on the other. You'd think hatred is a strong word until you see the crowd at a game like that.

We won the game – a fundraiser like that isn't the most competitive arena in the world – and then we headed down for a drink to a bar in Carrick; the Waterford people in there treated us like royalty because they had bragging rights for a few days.

That's what makes the GAA, those kinds of rivalries. They can get out of hand the odd time, but in general it's that desire to get one over on the neighbours – and the dread when you realize they're going to get it over on you – that drives inter-county players from bordering counties. In Lismore, we're closer to Youghal and Cork; in Waterford city, it's the Kilkenny side. In Carrick, obviously, it's Tipperary; but a few lads would probably confess that, no matter what part of the county they're from, they get a kick out of beating Tipp!

On the other side of the coin there's a guy like Liam Sheedy, the current Tipperary manager. I suppose it's a sign of my age that the guys I marked once upon a time are the managers on the sideline now. As a player he was definitely one of the toughest you could mark. He had his position in corner-back and would never say a word to you, which is odd when you see the passion he shows as a manager on the line. He really wears his heart on his sleeve.

The Munster final of 2002 didn't turn out the way Babs and Co. predicted. Ken got seven points from play, Flynn was terrific, Tony got on the end of a long Brenner puck-out and scored a goal. Eoin McGrath was outstanding. The lads were all heroes and we won a first Munster title in almost forty years in Páirc Uí Chaoimh.

I was happy enough to get on at the end, because everyone was playing so well, but I was only on the field for two minutes. I didn't feel part of it. I have no *meas* on the medal and couldn't tell you where it is at home.

I was delighted for Fergal Hartley, who soldiered for years – and felt sorry for Seanie Cullinane and Stephen Frampton, who didn't even get that day out, having been left off the panel by Justin that year. But I didn't feel I'd made a contribution myself.

Nicky English was managing Tipp and he came in after the game to wish us well, but the dressing rooms are so small in Cork that I was togging out in another room when he was talking and I couldn't hear him.

We had a dinner after the final in Cork but it was more alcohol than dinner. On the way back to Waterford, Peter

Queally made a call – he was based in Youghal with the Gardaí – and a squad car came out to meet us as we reached Youghal Bridge and stopped the traffic. We got off the bus and walked the cup across the bridge into Waterford. I remember it well, I had Micheál White up on my shoulders. Some steroids would have come in handy just then.

It was an incredible feeling, when we were rolling along the road to Waterford, looking out the bus window at the cars full of Waterford people passing us, or driving up behind us blowing their horns, showing us their colours. They'd waited so long for a Munster title, and now we had it . . . When we got to Dungarvan there was a crowd of about ten thousand people waiting for us in the Square. We were introduced on the stage, but as I say, I'd played a bit part, as a sub, rather than made a full contribution, and I felt embarrassed being introduced to the crowd. I would have given everything to have started.

I've never seen such celebrations, before or since. It was as if people felt free after waiting the guts of forty years to see Waterford win another Munster title.

I headed to my local, Paddy Foley's, then met up with the lads and went off to Lawlor's and the nightclubs. The following day we hit Jack Meade's, Hartley's father's spot – a prime spot – and then for Waterford city. More celebrations.

The Tuesday after the 2002 Munster final, myself and Chicken planned to go for a few drinks down in west Waterford. By the evening we were wondering about our next port of call. We gave Peter Queally a shout and he collected us, but we didn't head anywhere straight away – he brought us up home and his father Richie, God rest him, had a big feed waiting for us.

It mightn't sound like the most glamorous memory, but there was something unforgettable about it. A few of us sitting down, having the banter among ourselves, passing the spuds around the table, laughing and watching the Munster final we'd won the previous Sunday, the contrast between the crowds and the noise in Páirc Uí Chaoimh and the quiet enjoyment of Richie Queally's company. We had great nights out on the back of winning the Munster championship. That was a great day to have on the back of it.

Did we overdo those celebrations? I don't think so, but it's true it was hard to get fired up again for the All-Ireland series after being toasted the length and breadth of the county. Justin was telling us the whole time, 'Don't get carried away, there are bigger games to play yet.' He was good that way – he'd look to the bigger picture the whole time and try to keep our focus.

He told us to stay away from the media as well, but that was sometimes an issue within the team. He'd tell us not to give an interview, but he'd give plenty of them himself, and of course we noticed. Lads would go to him and say, 'Look, I want to do an interview with such and such a person,' and he'd knock them back. He'd say to players, 'Watch what you're saying and box clever, because they'll lead you up the garden path and hang you out to dry afterwards.'

He was right to an extent, because you could talk the talk and end up not walking the walk – though in honesty I can't remember the last time a GAA player said something as harmful as guaranteeing he'd win the next game. I never let myself down like that. I'd always be careful not to build myself up too much in the press or anything.

The reality is that if you're asked to give an interview, it can be a help to a player in his job or in getting a job. Managers are aware of that, or at least they should be.

In 2009, I was offered several hundred euro to do a newspaper interview in Dublin, and Davy Fitzgerald wouldn't let me do it. That's a lot of money to turn down, and it was frustrating when the guy saying no was involved in the media himself, as Davy was.

I don't have any problem with anyone in the media: my attitude is they're doing their job the same as I do mine, and whether I play well or not, it's not affected by the media. Some guy gives his opinion on the game, so what? I've been criticized, but what about it? If I don't play well, that's my own fault.

That's not to say the media aren't irresponsible from time to time. You don't have to be a genius to see where some reporters are trying to lead you with certain questions – if, for instance, a former manager is now in charge of your next opponents. No player is going to go off on a rant and say, 'You can write this, that I'll get three goals the next time out.' I don't know why they bother to ask, but I suppose they probably feel if they don't ask they'll never know.

It's more worrying for me when you see hurlers and footballers getting rated out of ten after games. That's a pretty unfair level of nitpicking. You see the ratings out of ten for soccer teams and they're rarely as harsh as they are for GAA teams. In fact, if you look at the ratings for Irish rugby teams, whether the Irish team or the provincial sides, they're never that harsh. Some of the GAA reporters might want to bear that in mind from time to time.

We played Clare in the All-Ireland semi-final and I didn't start in that game either. I came on and won a couple of frees, and it was frustrating not to get more of a run. We started well but faded, and Clare showed their experience, keeping in touch with us throughout and then going ahead as the game drew to a close.

We felt we weren't that great on the sideline that day, and that became a recurring issue with Justin – that he wouldn't make a substitution until late in the game, as though he had his mind made up that he was going to rely on the lads he'd picked to start, or as if breaking up the team he'd picked would be some kind of admission he'd made a mistake. As a result, in most of our games, unless there were injuries, most of the changes were made late.

There was also a fairly controversial incident in that game, when Clare's Gerry Quinn got his hand broken off the ball. I wasn't aware of that until after the game and I didn't see what happened. (I don't want to sound like Arsene Wenger here!)

It became a bit of a media sensation, the Quinn injury. Though there were the usual few dozen TV cameras in Croke Park for the game, they missed what had happened, and there was a lot of huffing and puffing about what the player responsible for the injury should do.

I remember that there was a lot of loose talk and sneaky finger-pointing when it came to the man who had supposedly caused the injury, but I didn't know then what happened and I haven't found out since.

I do know that the Waterford player who was blamed for it had a rough enough time himself after the game. He got hate mail from Clare and there were letters sent to his club asking them to expel him.

Justin was very good in the dressing room. He'd have the homework done well beforehand. We'd train on Tuesday, and then on Thursday he'd go through the opposition, player by player. Man for man, for instance, he'd always say Waterford were better hurlers than Cork. He might say, 'Lads, look at the six Cork forwards and the six Waterford forwards; if I was picking a team that combined Cork and Waterford there might only be two Cork forwards on that team.' (Nobody ever asked which two Waterford forwards he'd drop, mind you.)

Justin had some luck as well, compared to Gerald. He had more options, for one thing. My cousin Eoin Kelly came in and could wear any number from eight to fifteen and play outstandingly well. In fact, he's probably the best individual hurler in Ireland, never mind Waterford. This fella has everything. Speed, skill, strength – ask Shane O'Neill after the goal he got in this year's drawn Munster final – ability to strike off left and right side, vision. He's out of this world – one of those players who's so good he can be discouraging to play with.

One spring we were up in Ennis playing Clare in the league. It was a bad day for me: I was at full-forward and couldn't get a ball into my hand for love or money. Forget about scoring. After twenty minutes I couldn't remember what a *sliotar* looked like.

Eoin was sent on instead of me and in ten minutes he had four points scored – off his left and right, from every angle and distance. His striking is so clean you'd want to put your own hurley away; he's gone to Passage now from Mount Sion, but if he'd stayed with Mount Sion they'd definitely have another few counties won.

Eoin McGrath, Ken's brother, could double up as a busy corner-forward or workaholic in midfield. Eoin Murphy was on the fringes of the team as a wing-forward when Justin arrived; within a couple of years he was the All-Star corner-back.

John Mullane became a huge part of the team. Mull is a ferocious man to train, and on the field he's the best corner-forward in the business, but when we all head out he's another man who's always in the thick of it.

Once when Justin was in charge we went to Ballycastle in Antrim for a training weekend and played the Antrim county team on the last night. Afterwards the management said we could have a few drinks, so we all headed to a GAA club nearby. Fast forward an hour or two and Mullane is up on the stage, taking the microphone off the singer they had in for the night. Starts off with a few rebel songs and gets the whole place singing along, bouncing around the stage leading the sing-song with the come-all-yes. They couldn't get enough of him singing, and he couldn't get enough of him. I'd say there's another career there when he hangs up his boots. Personally, I think that weekend away won the 2002 Munster final.

Justin also had good leaders. Hartley would talk in the dressing room before games, and he was outstanding. Desperate dress sense, but a great leader, particularly in the dressing room.

12

We made a good effort at retaining the Munster title in 2003, though a lot of people won't remember the details. For instance, we took Limerick in the Munster semi-final, which went to a replay, but the game wasn't broadcast on television because RTÉ had some kind of health and safety issue putting cameras up on the cranes around the stadium. As a result many people missed three of the greatest goals I've ever seen; if that game had been broadcast on television the man responsible would have more than one All-Star, definitely.

Flynn – who else? I wasn't the only one who thought so, either – Justin said the same at the time and compared Flynn to Christy Ring, which was some praise for a Corkman to give.

For myself it wasn't a great year. I knew I was down the pecking order, which was brought home to me in the Munster final.

I have a very strong memory of that Munster final and how it ended. Why wouldn't I? I had a ringside seat, perched on the sideline.

With a few minutes left and the game in the melting-pot, Justin and the selectors put on Paul O'Brien of Tallow, a good player but a small man, at wing-forward. At that stage we were three points up, and I would have thought that the obvious move would be to put on a big man who'd win the ball and hold possession in the Cork half of the field, a tactical switch I would have advocated by clearing my throat and pointing at my own chest.

Unfortunately, when a ball came down to the right-half-forward position, right in front of us, Mark Prendergast of Cork blew Paul out of the way and drove the ball eight yards down the field, right on top of Cork's Joe Deane and Brian Greene. For a small man Joe was brilliant at just playing the hurley from behind under the dropping ball, a little tip to get the ball to come all the way through to him, and he did just that to Greener, grabbed the ball and got a goal. The decisive score: Cork tagged on the points to win, but it was Deano's goal that gave them the impetus to get over the finishing line.

At the final whistle my uncle Donal came down from the stand and said to me, 'Tell him [Justin] to fuck off and pack in the hurling.' I didn't, but I went up to Justin and the selectors and asked what I'd been doing wrong. Alan Browne was making his victory speech as we were talking, his Cork accent echoing around Semple Stadium.

'We're the management,' said Justin.

'I respect that totally,' I said. 'But can you tell me what I'm doing wrong?'

They couldn't answer me, and I ended up just walking away.

On the bus back after the match the lads were asking me why I wasn't brought on. I couldn't give them an answer. I felt the game was crying out for someone to hold the ball up – but you can't do that if you're sitting in the dug-out.

Donal's anger was easily explained: he felt that I was good enough to start, which was fair enough – I felt the same way myself – but he also felt that by not giving me a run in the Munster final, when Waterford should have been looking for something different to break up the game, they were signalling to me that my race was run at inter-county level.

I didn't think so. I felt Justin had had success in 2002 with the team he'd picked, and that he was always going to give them a chance to play themselves out of contention, if you like. My chance would come.

But it was hard, not starting. I'd made the wing-forward position my own in 1998, and felt I'd done well in the couple of years before Justin came in. I contributed from play and usually won a few frees in every game, troubling opposition half-backs with my ability to win the ball in the air.

The thought of quitting popped up once or twice, but whether I was foolish or just optimistic, I always felt I'd get another shot, that I was good enough to get a run in the team again, and that when I did I'd make it impossible for the selectors to ignore me.

It didn't improve in the qualifiers, when we were edged out by Wexford in Nowlan Park. We were flying it until Mullane picked up an eye injury, and we fell away badly after that. Wexford smelt the weakness and put us away; they could be ruthless if they felt they had a chance. This was my first championship start under Justin McCarthy and only for Damien Fitzhenry I could have got a couple of goals.

My own experiences against them went a few years further back: I remember a league game years ago down in Walsh Park, marking Liam Dunne when he was still playing centre-back for them. It would have been after 1996, when he was blamed by almost everybody in the country for taking Gary Kirby out of it early on in the All-Ireland final. I was wary enough of him and where he had the hurley.

At one stage a ball dropped between us – me at six foot three and him at five foot seven. I went full stretch to get the ball and got an unmerciful slap down across the hand from Liam, his hurley flying into pieces.

'For fuck sake, Liam,' I said, 'what are you at?'

'The ball was there – the ball was there,' he said.

'It's there all right,' I said. 'It's about three feet away from where you pulled.'

Sometimes I wonder do smaller fellas like to take it out on big fellas, because Liam took plenty out on me that day.

Then a few years ago I was coming through Dungarvan when I bumped into him on the street – we had a great chat, stayed talking for ages. And I got away without a sore hand.

The big change early in 2004 was Gerry Fitzpatrick coming in full-time to take over the physical training. He had held a few sessions back in 1995 and 1996, but in 2004 he fell in full-time with us. He was a huge help. He's an international basketball coach with vast experience, and the sessions changed totally.

At the start of the year he gave us a heavy programme of

weights, but he also brought us down to Waterford Institute of Technology to show us how to lift those weights properly. We had no excuse. After that it was up to the individual to do the programme, but Gerry would know by looking at each of us whether or not we were doing it. He often said to me, 'I know by the look of you you're doing it – you're looking wicked strong.'

But Gerry was more than that. We could talk to him about work, about preparation – and about parts of the build-up to a big game that didn't relate obviously to either work or preparation. He'd say to us, 'Have three or four bottles of beer three weeks before the match. Don't be going cracked on the beer the night before.' He'd advise us on our diet. If we had any kind of a problem he was available to talk on the phone all the time.

I couldn't credit him enough for how we developed. The difference between him and Colm Bonnar, who'd handled the physical training when he was a selector, was that Colm was maybe too nice to give out to someone if they weren't putting it in physically. He wouldn't fuck you out of it, but Gerry would: 'Dan, you're not putting it in tonight. Work harder.' Or worse.

He often travelled in the same car as Paul Flynn to training, roared at Flynn for the entire training session – and then sat back into the car with him for the lift home afterwards. I often wondered what the conversations in the car were like. Or whether they just played the radio as a compromise.

Flynn had it all in his wrists: he could literally make the ball do anything he wanted. But he wasn't as good to train as some of the other lads on the panel. He made a huge effort for years but it probably got to a point where he was relying on his experience rather than his fitness to survive. I often ran the laps with him and tried to drive him on, but after a while I'd have to speed up or I'd be codding myself.

There was another element to the Flynn situation in that that we would probably have relied on him to the extent that it was a problem. He was like a get-out-of-jail-free card: if the game was even enough and you were looking for a go-ahead score or an equalizer, the easiest thing in the world to do was to look for Flynn to work his magic.

And he did it more often than not. You could trust him with the late free, or the tough effort from play standing out on the sideline. But the downside was that the team was reliant on him. Too reliant. Other players didn't get used to testing themselves and finding out if they had the guts to go for an equalizer with two minutes gone in injury time, or to stand over a 21-metre free when we were two points down with time almost up.

I think it might have been part of Justin's plan to reduce the team's dependence on Flynn that I got back on to the first fifteen. I certainly remember him saying to me early on in 2004, 'Don't always be looking up to Paul Flynn. Remember who you are.'

I understood what he was trying to tell me. I had trained in 2002 and 2003 in the group with Flynn and Eoin Kelly, but that meant I was in a comfort zone. In retrospect, that could have been part of the reason Justin wasn't starting me: that he felt I was keeping afloat rather than trying to improve. They say when you train a team to look at the lads in the middle of the bunch, because the lads at the back can't go any faster, and neither can the lads in the front, but the boys in the middle are doing just enough not to catch the trainer's eye. And in 2002–3 I might have been one of those lads in the middle of the bunch.

I moved into the group with bigger lads in 2004 – the likes of James Murray, lads who'd hit you hard and who drove themselves hard. That helped. It improved my fitness and my strength, which were also benefiting from Gerry Fitzpatrick's involvement. It all came together, and I think Justin noticed that I'd stayed on the panel, stayed working.

We got to the league final in 2004 against Galway, up in Limerick, after a good campaign. We lost fairly heavily; Justin tried Eoin McGrath at corner-back, taking a chance, and it didn't work out for us.

It worked out for me, though. I was fit and strong, I'd trained hard, and I enjoyed the league final. I got 1–3 from play and nearly got another goal before half-time when I got in behind the defence, but I kicked the ball, it screwed off the side of my boot and went wide.

I took a lot out of that game. If you asked a GAA anorak they'd probably struggle to remember anything about it, but it was a big plus for me to score that much in a national final. It gave me confidence – no surprise there – but it also confirmed what I'd thought all along: that I deserved my place and was more than good enough. Getting a nice total like that freed me up. If I could do it in a league final, I could do it in any game.

Clare thought they only had to show up for the Munster championship quarter-final. They had most of their top players still, but we were different from the Waterford team that had been squeezed out by Cork in the Munster final in 2003. With Gerry's involvement we were physically stronger and fitter, and while it had been disappointing to lose the league final, our run of games during the spring suggested to us that we were on the right track. We only had to show that in the championship.

I was certainly confident and strong, and so were the rest of the lads, despite the loss to Galway. We were bringing good form into the Clare game and were underdogs, which never hurts. We had everything right going into that game. Justin and Gerry were telling us to enjoy it. We also had a plan.

I was named at wing-forward but Justin told me to go where I wanted to go. That was the great master plan we had – that Justin basically trusted me to weigh up the games as they were progressing, to take the odd chance and drift in behind the opposition full-back line in search of a goal chance.

It helped that I was on the same wing as Mullane, because we had a great understanding of each other's play. As the game would develop, I knew he would be coming out the field looking for the ball, and when he did I'd just ghost in behind the full-back line.

On paper it looks so obvious that you'd imagine a senior inter-county wing-back would cop on to it immediately, but they rarely did. As a ploy it worked with almost every wing-back because they'd be unsure where I was going – corner-forward, full-forward, or what – and they'd be worried about leaving a gap behind them. If a manager saw his left-half-back missing, he'd go ballistic – it'd be like hanging a sign off the sideline flag saying, 'Attack here.'

Just about the only defender who never bought it was JJ Delaney – the best of them, unfortunately. All the rest were confused because they weren't sure where I was going to end up, so they didn't know whether to stick or twist.

That was the benefit of having played the league game against Galway. I'd seen that their defence wasn't sure what to do with me, so I knew it would work. When it came to Clare, they tried Conor Plunkett and Gerry Quinn on me, but that didn't bother me. I was in the zone.

The first goal came when the ball drifted in over Brian Lohan, just beyond him, to me. Eoin Kelly had taken a pot shot for a point but the effort died, only to fall into my lap. I got it on the edge of the square, shortened my grip and buried it. I saw on the video later that if Lohan had made contact with the kick he drew on me as I wound up he'd have driven me up on to the terrace, or higher, but he missed.

Seeing the ball hit the back of the net lifted a weight off my shoulders, cliché though that sounds. I hadn't played in 2002, hadn't much action in 2003, and now I had a goal. In the Munster championship.

I caught my jersey and kissed the crest, I was so delighted. That was the start of it – but it was just something that happened. I was so relieved.

A lot of people have criticized us since then for getting pumped up when we get a goal. You'd imagine we should all still be wearing cloth caps like they did fifty years ago. If people don't like it, fine. If they'd celebrate a different way, that's fine too. But what makes me laugh is some kind of suggestion that what we're doing when we kiss the crest of our jersey is either (a) nothing to do with hurling or (b) just aping something that goes on in soccer.

As for (a), I'm quite sure that in the fifties the players were told by those who played forty years before them that what they were doing had nothing to do with hurling. To answer (b), I can only say that I'm not aping any celebration I've seen in a soccer game; I can prove it because after kissing the Waterford crest I've never transferred to another county in time for the following season!

I don't tell anybody how to behave – what's right for them to do or what's wrong. And if you score a goal in a Munster hurling final and you don't want to celebrate it, that's fine – that's your choice. For me, though, that would be impossible. It's such an incredible sensation to see the net billow when you hit the ball, the split second before the crowd erupts. You don't have to go crazy, or lose your focus, but you've just put yourself in the middle of Irish sports history.

Who wouldn't celebrate that?

The critics miss the most important point, though; we do it because it happens naturally. There's no plan involved; there never was.

I didn't get carried away after that goal – the game was far from over – but the relief was huge after the couple of seasons I'd had. It meant I'd been right to hang in there. It was great for my family, too. I'd had plenty of abuse the previous couple of years, people saying, 'Take that Shanahan off, he's gone,' on the rare occasions I started, and others shouting, 'Don't put him on,' when it looked like I was being brought on. I wouldn't hear it, obviously, but my family would have to listen to it. Bite the tongue.

So, a goal gives them a chance to relax and enjoy the game a bit more, as they don't have to listen to people bawling abuse at me.

The day got better and better for me. I got a second goal, which was as big a thrill as the first, but then it came into my head: *You've two goals scored. What would it be like to get a third?*

With time running out, I got a third for the hat-trick. The ball came back off the post, but I'd always face the goal and follow it in – you never know, there might only be one in twenty would come back to you, and that was one. I didn't make a great connection with the ball and it just dribbled over the line. When it did the Clare 'keeper turned back out the field to face his defenders. I saw in his eyes he was beat. I nearly jumped up on the terrace.

It was Davy Fitzgerald, of course, in goal for Clare that day. Like a lot of people, he annoyed me with the carry-on of slapping the bar with the hurley and jumping up and down. Anyone could be brave with Brian and Frank Lohan standing in front of them. But he was a good 'keeper. You could turn my attitude to him around as well, and say it was a tribute to him that I wanted to get a goal against him. Beating a 'keeper three times, particularly one of the best, was outstanding.

To give Davy his dues, at the final whistle he was man enough to walk out to me, shake my hand and wish me the best.

*

Me scoring the three goals was fantastic for my father, who's a quiet man – my uncles are quiet men too, but they'd react fairly quick if they heard someone abusing me. My phone was in the bottom of my gear bag, and it nearly melted with all the texts. Unbelievable.

Of course, I knew that plenty of people who were praising me in 2004 had been cutting strips off me in the pub and on the terraces before that. What those people don't realize is that every fella out on the field is doing his best. If it doesn't go for him, nobody knows it better than he does. He doesn't need some fool roaring abuse at him to remind him of the fact.

The best of all, of course, are the morons who'd be shouting for you to get taken off because you're useless until you get a score and you're a hero, the best in the world. Make sense of that.

People are entitled to their opinions; I have no problem with that. I have a problem with players being abused by lads full of cans up behind the goal who are just along for the drinking session. I wouldn't be innocent myself – I was that soldier. I well remember falling asleep one day at a Waterford game after a few drinks when I was a teenager, but I wasn't shouting abuse at the players.

As I said earlier, getting dog's abuse in the 1995 Munster minor final helped me, because I was used to that kind of abuse from a young age. The other side, though, is that I'd never go up on to the terraces once I finish up playing. I know that Pat Spillane said when he was badly injured and couldn't play for Kerry he'd go to games and be shocked by the abuse rained down on players by spectators, and I couldn't face that. I couldn't listen to some clown abuse Maurice or the lads; I know what they've gone through, I know they're doing their best, and not getting £100,000 a week for it.

The reward for beating Clare was a date with Tipperary in the Munster semi-final. Some reward. Some date.

That was a Munster championship day: a jam-packed stadium, baking heat, non-stop noise, two teams going hammer and tongs from start to finish. It was the full experience – including the crisis just before the throw-in.

Tony Browne cried off that morning, a massive blow at any time but against Tipp it could have been fatal. In a way, a big game like that isn't complete without that kind of thing, though – a late withdrawal, or a rumour of a late withdrawal. It's gas the way those rumours ripple out from the stadium in the couple of hours before throw-in, rolling down through the crowds. Not so gas when you're trying to get your head right to face Tipp, though.

Fair dues to the selectors, they pitched Brian Wall in for his debut and he had a great game, though there was another side to that selection, which I'll come back to later. The first ball he dealt with was a difficult one – a Tipp shot for a point came back off our post to Brian, but he took it on the bounce up off the ground, a very difficult ball to gather, and cleared it up the field. That little flash of skill showed he was ready, and it gave everyone else on the team confidence.

I got plenty of stick off the Tipperary crowd, not surprisingly: 'No goals for you today, Shanahan,' that kind of thing, just phrased a bit more colourfully.

Tipp had their homework done on the sideline about me, and it was clear they planned to deal with my runs, but I didn't need to make any on the blind side for my first goal.

In the first half we had a sideline cut, and as the ball was dropping in I could tell the Tipp player in front of me was gone up too early for it and wasn't going to get to it. Funny how that happens: despite all the preparation and all the planning, a player can make a simple error of timing, and just as you realize the ball is going to carry beyond him, he realizes it as well: he's mistimed his jump, and he's going to be punished for it.

I went up behind him, got it and buried it – it might have looked like me just blasting the ball, but I placed it to the side of Brendan Cummins in the Tipp goal. At that range, about seven or eight yards out, you just have to make sure you don't hit the 'keeper, and it'll rattle the onion bag.

When your luck is in, your luck is in. The proof of that was in the second goal I got. Our Eoin Kelly was outfield and mishit the ball – he was going for a point and the ball fell my way. I got the hurley to it and I was just able to reach it and flick it past Brendan Cummins.

I celebrated. Instead of heading back out the field I ran just in front of the Tipp supporters – it was at the Blackrock End in Páirc Uí Chaoimh, where all the Tipp crowd were, and I decided it was time to get a rise out of them, just for the craic.

If you've never run past ten thousand Tipperary people who are screaming for your blood, then it's an experience I'd heartily recommend.

Two touches, two goals. But confidence is a huge part of

that. The fact that I'd scored three goals in the previous match was a help, and so was the fact that Tipp were nervous. I could see it – their backs were looking around to check where I was, and from that day on they always had two players minding me whenever I played. I feed off that. Rather than intimidating me, it fills me with confidence. I start to believe, *Hey, they think I need two men to mind me. I'll give them something to worry about*.

For all of that, we looked beaten with time almost up. We were two points down but in crisis all over the field. Ken McGrath had had to go off injured. Flynn had been substituted. We were knocking on the door but we just didn't seem to have the key to get through.

Then Seamus Prendergast won the ball in the last minute and hit it in low to the full-forward line – a ground ball in towards the goal, the kind of delivery that brings slow defenders out in a cold sweat.

We had someone there to avail himself of it, but it wasn't me. The irony is that I'd have been in that exact spot nine times out of ten, coming across from the right corner, but I had moved outfield to draw the Tipp defenders with me. Paul O'Brien was the man making that run instead. Paul, remember, was the man blown over the sideline the previous year by Mark Prendergast of Cork, but did he make up for it against Tipp. He pulled on the ball from twenty yards and beat Brendan Cummins with a shot into the corner, which tells you just how good a ground stroke it was.

Cummins was in good form that day, too. He'd made an unbelievable save from Flynn not long before, diving up to the top corner to flick the ball around the post for a 65 – one of the best saves I've ever seen. Flynn had often said to me, 'I'd love to beat him' – a few forwards wouldn't be fond of Cummins, mind you: he'd be cocky enough on the field, as most 'keepers are, and as 'keepers they probably have to be. And in addition, Cummins can back it up. He's an outstanding goalie.

The goal was late, but it wasn't the last word that day. Tipp had another chance when Cummins landed his puck-out down in our defence, but Bryan Phelan came up with a little bit of skill, a little bit of magic that nobody remembers in comparison to Paul O'Brien's goal.

The ball was loose for a heartbeat in the half-back line, just skittering away from a knot of players, when Phelan intervened beautifully to break up that last attack – he flicked the loose ball up into his hand, an outrageous piece of skill. He cleared it down the field and the ref blew the final whistle.

The heat, the crowd in on top of us, Tipp getting the upper hand, Waterford winning with a goal in the last minute. That's not just the championship. That's the Munster championship.

The unfortunate footnote to the game is that it was Brian Wall's only start in the championship. Within the year he'd gone back to the Waterford footballers. He hadn't been getting a look in but, more significantly, he felt he didn't get any feedback on what he needed to improve – what he had to do in training or in games to ensure he would get a look in. He walked, which left us a capable player short.

We celebrated after that win. The funny thing is, Justin was never too bothered about us drinking, for a fella who didn't take a pint himself. He dealt with that kind of thing brilliantly. Other managers take that side of things very seriously but he was reasonably laid-back. He'd say, 'Relax, take it easy and don't go over the top.'

If I had a few drinks on the Sunday night after the game, that'd go into Monday afternoon and evening; and if it was three weeks to the next match you might hit Tuesday as well. We'd celebrate, but that'd be it – a few pints in Paddy Foley's in Dungarvan, then on to the Local Bar.

We needed to do it. There's a lot of talk about professionalism and the dedication that players have to show and so on, but a big championship game can hang over players' heads for weeks beforehand. There's talk at home, there's talk at work, there's pressure, they turn on the radio, or the television, and people are talking about it. Then on the day it all comes to a head and they have to blow off a bit of steam after it. They need to.

Most of the team takes a drink, and we have a bit of craic together. What else is it about? I'm talking about young fellas, most of them in their twenties, most of them single. What do you expect to happen?

Look at what happened with Tomas Ó Sé and Colm Cooper: they went drinking during the 2009 season but Kerry dealt with it in-house brilliantly. They suspended the two players internally, which meant a disciplinary procedure was used without going over the top and they went on to win the All-Ireland that year, with the two lads playing starring roles. I was lucky to meet some of the Kerry legends, the Ó Sé brothers, David Murphy, Tommy Griffin and the great Mikey Sheehy on a trip to the Cheltenham Races at

Shannon Airport. It was like I had known the lads all my life the way we got on. That to me is what the GAA is about.

That's the important thing: on every team you'll have a few fellas who take a drink, and out of them there'll probably be one or two who'll go over the top occasionally, but the important thing is how it is handled when it happens.

It would have happened with us too the odd time, but in fairness to Justin, he dealt with that aspect of management well.

Look at an example from the Premiership: Chelsea went on the beer after winning the title in 2010 even though they were down to play Portsmouth the following Saturday in the FA Cup – and they're professionals.

People read too much into drinking, and drink bans. Younger players can't do anything. If a lad's seen going into a pub and he has a Lucozade, people say, 'Oh, he's having vodka and Lucozade.' If you're seen out around the town at all in the evening, then by the time the stories go round the following day, you were in the horrors.

People might wonder why I'm picking on that aspect of playing – or celebrating – but it seems to be a particular stick used to beat us with. Just because we'll have a night out after a game and enjoy it, unlike other counties, doesn't mean the whole team is staggering from one hangover to the next. We couldn't be, given what we've won in the last decade.

It was only after the goals went in against Tipp that I understood the pressure I was coming under myself. Even in the glass factory, my own pals were saying, 'Hey, will you do it again?' They were congratulating me, and one lad in the factory, Dave Long, had stuck up cuttings from the papers everywhere. That was fairly embarrassing, and I couldn't look at them in case people thought I had a big head.

Everyone was very supportive. Sometimes after a game they might say, 'Where were you yesterday in that game?' but by and large they were very good, especially when journalists would ring the factory to talk to me. I'd have the earphones on me, working away, and one of the lads would come up and tap me on the shoulder: 'Hey, there's a reporter on the phone there for you.'

That was a change for me, the sudden interest from the media after I'd been in the 'wilderness' for a couple of years. I'd guess I was often an interview target because I was probably more recognizable than a lot of lads, simple as that. I wouldn't have thought I was more famous or anything. Anything but.

I said earlier that Justin had his fifteen to twenty players picked out, and when he started taking my hurleys away I knew I'd moved into that group. But I'd criticize him for not knowing some lads on the panel well enough. One night he had Ian O'Regan, a goalkeeper, playing corner-forward in a mixed match – it wasn't unlike the night that drove Brendan Landers over the top and off the panel. That brought home to Ian just how important he was in the plans for the team.

Gerry Fitzpatrick was the man who dealt with the players. He was far more than a trainer: he was part psychologist as well. And he was needed, because there was wicked pressure on us in the run-up to the Munster final against Cork.

For me, the pressure centred on where I'd be playing,

wing- or centre-forward. On the day I started on the wing, with Seán Óg next to me, but he was gone across to right-half-back after the anthem, before the ball was even thrown in, and John Gardiner came over to me. I was happy with that: Gardiner is a decent player but it's hard to defend against a good puck-out, and we had a great system going at that time.

Stevie Brenner was in goal for us that day and while he had a huge puck-out, which was a fantastic weapon for us when we won the 2002 Munster championship, his shot-stopping wasn't quite at the same level. That was proved in the 2004 Munster final, when Garvan McCarthy's goal trickled between his legs.

But he still had that awesome puck-out, and he landed them right down on me. I caught the first three balls he dropped into me, and I could see Gardiner was getting frustrated that he couldn't get into the game. It got to him. Late in the first half we were tussling away in the corner and I said to him, 'John, would you ever go away and play the game?' as we were coming out. He responded with 'Fuck off,' or something similar, and then he went for me.

I pushed my hand out and gave him a poke in the face – and he went down straight away in a heap. The ref came in and booked both of us. I couldn't take it to heart too much. I was on top, and as far as I was concerned he was trying to get me into trouble and he went down fairly easily, but I wouldn't bear a grudge about it.

It's probably easy for me to say that because I got my own back not too long after. Eoin Kelly, again, took the shot from out the field and he mishit it, again. I was between Gardiner and Diarmuid O'Sullivan, and I knew as soon as the ball left Eoin's hurley that it was going to drop right for me.

The advantage was with me: with two fellas picking you up often neither of them knows who's going for the ball, and Dónal Óg, behind us in the goal, didn't call it. I caught the ball and turned left and let fly, and it hit the back of the net.

There was no celebrating that day. Justin had warned us off doing that and to stay focused. I enjoyed that one, though. Catching the ball with the two lads there and beating Dónal Óg? You get a goal in a Munster final, you're going to enjoy it.

When I got back out to wing-forward I had different company. Donal O'Grady had shifted Seán Óg over on me. Seán Óg is someone I've had many the battle with, and I've always found him extremely tough to mark. Over the years, we've met loads of times, and he's a lovely fella. When he spoke in Irish as captain of Cork in the All-Ireland final in 2005, it was brilliant.

But I was never nervous about marking Seán Óg – I always loved to have a bit of a chat with him, to see if I could put him off – and I don't think he gets the credit he deserves for coming back from that bad car accident to become one of the best wing-backs in Ireland.

You don't realize, either, what others make of him until you share a dressing room with him. We won the Railway Cup in 2007, and one of the matches was played below in Fermoy. To see the queue of people looking for autographs from Seán Óg was incredible. I signed a few autographs myself but it was all about Seán Óg and he stayed on to sign them all.

*

The atmosphere was good in the dressing room at half-time. We were doing well in a tough game but Justin said that a few fellas had to buck up their ideas in the second half. That was meant for Paul Flynn. He was cat in the first half and could have been taken off, but he really turned it on in the second half. And we needed him.

John Mullane was getting a bit of a name for himself as a predator up front, a forward who had to be watched. He'd scored three goals in the previous year's Munster final, and Cork weren't going to let him get another three against them. A couple of minutes into the second half, he got entangled with a Cork player, who ended up on the ground. When the referee consulted with his umpires Mullane was sent off. Down to fourteen men.

We had to reorganize ourselves, because Cork left Diarmuid O'Sullivan as the free man. They took a few quick puck-outs and we copped that fairly quickly and shut them down, but they were definitely coming back into it as the half wore on.

Then I won a free off Seán Óg. I'd won the ball in the air and turned him and he pulled me back as I headed for goal: it was a definite free. I jogged into the edge of the square and when I looked back out the field, I saw Flynn take a little cheeky glance as he stood over the ball. I was standing in front of Diarmuid O'Sullivan and Dónal Óg to make a nuisance of myself. I felt if Flynn dipped the free in I'd at least swing the hurley at it to cause a problem. I don't think Sully enjoyed marking me because I was taller than him, and Dónal Óg would have had to move to the side to see the ball around me.

Flynn lined up the free and put pace and a dip on the ball and it rattled the corner of the net. I tried to get a touch to it to put the defence off, but I don't think it was needed. His strike was that good.

Did he mean it? It was a Paul Flynn special. We had seen it often enough in training, or in Waterford club games against Ballygunner. Of course he meant it.

After that it was backs to the wall for us, but we upped the game, as fourteen men always do. The goal was a huge boost, and it rattled Cork because they were nervous of conceding a free within fifty yards of their goal.

We covered huge ground up front and the defenders were as good at the other end. With time almost up, we were hanging on by our fingernails when Cork launched one last attack. Ken McGrath won a huge ball for us, catching it over Sully's head, and when he was fouled coming out, the game was as good as over.

That was probably the biggest day of my life, sports-wise. The year I'd had – Galway in the league final, Clare, Tipp, then Cork – meant I had seven goals to my name in a couple of months, six in the Munster championship. It was out of this world. I headed for the dressing room and just soaked up the atmosphere.

In a way I felt I'd come back. The previous two seasons, 2002 and 2003, I'd spent in the wilderness, forcing myself to stay positive and to bide my time. I'd scored five goals in the two previous games and one in the Munster final, which gave me a fairly healthy balance in my account. Sitting in the dressing room, accepting the handshakes and slaps on the back was pretty sweet.

We didn't celebrate the way we did in 2002, though. There was a bit of a cloud over Mullane: he was distraught and saying he'd let the players down because he'd been sent off, but there was no shortage of teammates telling him, 'Not at all' – and they were right. It could happen to the best of players.

Mullane's situation wasn't a distraction for the All-Ireland semi-final against Kilkenny. It was cut and dried long before the game that he wasn't playing, so we were used to that idea, even though there were suggestions that businessmen in Waterford would fund some kind of appeal to the High Court to get him freed up for it. But Mull said he'd take his punishment, and he did. I know a few people, like GAA President Sean Kelly, talked a lot about how much they admired his stance in accepting the GAA's ruling. A pity some other counties wouldn't learn from that.

I marked JJ Delaney that day. He's a fantastic hurler, but I feel he gets away with a lot of fouls. My experience is that when the ball is coming down he'll climb up on your back; but somehow he gets away with it. In my opinion, JJ's a spoiler – he doesn't care if he doesn't hit the ball so long as you don't hit it. That's fair enough: if you're a defender you're there to hold your man scoreless rather than to entertain the spectators with your skill. I've marked hurlers from every county but Kilkenny are different. Hurley around your neck, playing your hurley instead of the ball . . . I'd love to have JJ playing wing-forward against us; I'd enjoy playing wing-back on him.

That day we'd have been destroyed only for Flynn. He got

fourteen points, and if he'd had someone else with him we'd have won. Iggy (Ian O'Regan) made his debut that day for us in goal, and he was a confident lad, but he got a bit nervous on the day, not surprisingly. Playing your first championship game in Croke Park, in an All-Ireland semi-final, would test anyone's nerve.

We lost: another close game in Croke Park gone against us. So close yet so far again. Nothing is as bad as coming off the field in Croke Park beaten. I wasn't happy. We'd been good in Munster but we'd been quietened in Croke Park. Again.

I won an All-Star award that year. The year had gone well; I'd scored six goals so half suspected I'd be nominated. But I didn't know I'd win one. I picked up a Player of the Month award as well that year for June, with Vodafone; we had a good day and I was given a free phone, though I left it in the taxi afterwards! I had to leg it down the street shouting at the cabbie to stop. Classy. I had my parents with me that day and we knocked great craic out of it.

The All-Stars function was different. Any time we've gone up, the Waterford lads always go to the same corner of the bar, and we hammer it. And we hammered it that night. It's great meeting the likes of the northern lads, that's a huge highlight for me – lads like Sean Cavanagh or Stevie McDonnell, who are awesome players, and it's nice to meet up somewhere you can have a chat instead of just rushing past each other in Croke Park after a game. They're always fierce interested in hurling, too.

13

We had Cork in the Munster semi-final in 2005 too, but the year didn't go half as well for us. Injuries were a huge problem; you could say they crippled us in 2005. Flynn could barely walk against Cork, though he got a goal with a fantastic stroke off the ground from twenty yards.

So did I. Eoin mishit a 65 in the second half; I'd have scored a lot fewer goals if he'd hit the ball better or more accurately. The Cork lads stood off me, and I caught it near the square. I fell with half of Cork on my back and the ball broke from my hand, but I kept my head: I knew if I made contact that I was so near to the goal I had a chance. I pulled on the loose ball and it went in.

This kept my average up; in fact, I've had an average of a goal in every game from the time Justin started, up to 2008. If you were guaranteed a goal from every forward every day you'd be quite happy, but my average didn't help us to win that day.

What made it doubly disappointing was that we had Fergal Hartley back, but in the wrong position. He'd retired in 2003 but Justin had coaxed him back on to the panel, and he'd worked hard to get himself match fit. However, Justin tried to make a full-back out of Hartley that year, one of the best centre-backs we've ever had. I still think that if he'd put him back in his old position we might have done better against Cork in those two games, and I wouldn't blame Hartley when he packed it in after the 2005 season.

(I should also put on the record that Hartley's dress sense has improved significantly since the old days. Then again, there was no way it could get worse.)

We had to face the qualifiers, which was a knock-out format, and our first opponents were Offaly.

It didn't get much better for us. We played them up in Carlow, and the only thing I'd take out of that game, apart from the win, was marking Brian Whelehan in his last game for Offaly. It was a challenge for me to play against such a good hurler. He was a class act and I have huge respect for him. Clearly he was at the end of a long and fantastic career by the time I crossed swords with him, but the flashes of genius were still there – the touch, the instant control.

I made sure I got his jersey at the end of the game. It was a good one to get.

We folded again in Croke Park that year in the All-Ireland quarter-final. Cork beat us in a game that was dead enough all the way through until Brian Corcoran got a goal late on to win it. I got one after Flynn deliberately mishit the ball taking a 21-metre free. He'd do it in training, and he did it then in Croke Park. He'd gone for goal from a free early on and Dónal Óg had batted it back out, so when we won another free the Cork players expected him to blast it again. He didn't. He put it into the ground, they stopped it and it rolled out. I reacted quickest, coming in to pull on the ball.

That was no satisfaction. Cork went on to win that All-Ireland and that makes a difference. Once again, I was in Waterford watching the game on TV and saying, 'Why aren't we there?'

I didn't go up for the game, though some of the Waterford lads would make a weekend of it. I headed for Paddy Foley's that day and maybe had a bet with someone on the first goal, but that's no consolation, having a pint and a punt in Dungarvan when you really want to be in Croke Park.

Clinton Hennessy was parachuted in for that All-Ireland quarter-final in 2005 – some game to make your championship debut in. I can still see Cork dropping the first ball into the square, obviously trying to find out how his nerves were and whether he'd be up to the test of commanding the area in front of his goal in Croke Park. He came out, fielded the ball and drove it ninety yards back down the pitch. He was up to it that day and he's been up to it ever since.

He and the other Ardmore lads, Declan and Seamus Prendergast, are all close. They mightn't have a reputation as party animals, but if you're looking for a bit of craic on the Monday after a game, they're the lads to look for. It's always the quiet ones.

There was no dissatisfaction with Justin at that time. He'd brought us on, he'd improved us, and there was no group of players who were unhappy. But we were conscious that we hadn't won a big game in Croke Park since 1998 and Galway. We could beat the best of them in Thurles, but Croke Park was different. It was becoming an issue for us and we knew we'd have to address if it we were ever going to progress. Being kings of Munster and pushovers in Dublin wasn't a legacy any of us were interested in.

I had concerns off the field that year too. It was clear that Waterford Crystal's business had started going down, and you'd know it when you were sent off to the packing area. The union rep was good and advised me to take what I could get and go, so I took the redundancy package that we were offered in 2005.

Fair dues to Paddy Joe Ryan then, the Waterford county board chairman: he came up to me in Fraher Field after that and said he might have something for me. He asked if I'd be interested in driving a lorry for Comeragh Oil, and I said I would, but I was saying to myself, *Christ, I took two attempts to get my driving test with the car, how long am I going to take learning to drive a lorry?*

I took a chance and it worked out. I met Sean Murphy and Catherine Barron and they interviewed me for the job, two great people. As they put it, they were offering me a job for life, and I nearly took their hands off.

To learn the ropes I was put in with a great man, Nicky Donovan. I was in the lorry with him for over six months, took lessons and passed the test on the first attempt. I couldn't believe it. Nicky and David Ryan taught me everything. All the lads at Comeragh are great workers, great mates, and I'll always be grateful they gave me the job – and the business I got from Lismore, and from lads I worked with in the glass factory, was great. I'd like to think I repaid Comeragh Oil's faith in me.

People think it's a soft job – it's no soft job. During the winter you might have to make forty or fifty calls in a day, but in the summer it's quieter, and they're very good to look after me with time off for games. I couldn't speak highly enough of Paddy Joe Ryan for that chance, and of the lads in Comeragh Oil. I have wicked time for all of them.

One great thing about the job is meeting people on the road. Some of the customers know nothing whatsoever about hurling, but others want to talk about nothing else. I have no problem with lads talking hurling, as long as they don't start cutting my teammates to pieces. Everyone has their own opinion, but I draw the line sometimes if a fella is out of line about my teammates. If a fella is working twelve or thirteen hours a day, then how dare anyone knock him for giving up his spare time to train and represent his county?

Some people have done that and I've put them in their place, but the vast majority of people are hugely encouraging – the number of times I've heard 'good luck' is unbelievable, and the young lads looking for autographs are fantastic. I always try to help out there, because my father always told me, 'It's nice to be nice.' It's a great job, and I love it; it's a major part of my life.

14

At least I had that stability in work facing 2006, though with Waterford our preparations weren't too hectic approaching the championship. Going into our first game – the Munster semi-final against Tipp in Páirc Uí Chaoimh – Mullane had a hand injury, our own Eoin Kelly was suspended after giving a fella a slap across the arse in a league game against Offaly, while I got food poisoning the week before that game and was weak as water.

I shouldn't have played against Offaly, but it was difficult to tell Justin you couldn't play, even if you were genuinely sick. He wouldn't really take it on board: he'd just say, 'You'll get through it.' I'd been given an injection by our team doctor, Tom Higgins, before that Offaly game – not steroids or anything – but I had to come off anyway.

Anyone who's ever had food poisoning, an illness that involves spending a lot of time in the smallest room in the house – put it that way, with no further details – will know that you're in no shape to do anything other than lie in bed drinking fluids. Trying to get past some bear of a centre-back isn't recommended by any doctors as a cure, and it was no surprise when I got the call to come off.

I got some abuse from the stand as I walked to the sideline. From the Waterford crowd, of course. I had highlights in my hair then, and they were ribbing me over that. My brother James was at the game and he nearly lost the head with some of the beauties from Waterford who were there.

You'd do well to figure that one out: why would you go all the way up to Offaly just to abuse your own?

It was a bad day all round, then. I had to make the long march off, Eoin got sent off – and Offaly beat us out the gate. Not the greatest preparation for the championship game with Tipp in Páirc Uí Chaoimh.

Following Iggy's debut in 2004, we had another funny debut in 2006 when Denis Coffey was put in at corner-back against Tipperary. Denis is a tough player – Mullane and himself often had a fight in training; we'd see the two lads rolling around the ground up in the corner of Walsh Park while the rest of us were playing a mixed match. But it was a tall order to parachute him in for a Munster semi-final in Páirc Uí Chaoimh, a full house – and, most dangerous of all, an in-form opponent. Picking Denis was a punt from Justin that didn't work out.

He was marking Eoin Kelly, who had scored fourteen points in the previous round for Tipp against Limerick and won the Man of the Match award. Eoin is some player anyway, but he was in red-hot form that year. He scored 2–9 against us, one point more than he'd managed against Limerick.

At that rate, he would have been on course to get sixteen

points against Cork in the Munster final, but he didn't, because they organized their defence to bottle him up – they had Seán Óg lying deeper than he normally would, well back from his normal station at wing-back, to cut off the supply to him.

We didn't try anything like that with Eoin. We didn't even have our best man-marker on him. Justin had Eoin Murphy in the other corner – why didn't he put him on Kelly? The way the game went, he had to be switched over anyway after Kelly got his two goals, and he quietened him when he went over. It didn't make sense to me to have a defender on your team who'd always done well on the opposition's most dangerous forward and not to use him on that forward.

We would meet Tipp again later in the year after getting through the qualifiers, and a few people wondered whether Justin had that possibility in mind when we played them in Cork – that he was preparing us for a run through the qualifiers. I doubt it. The Munster championship is the Munster championship: no team goes out to lose a game in that competition, and it's always easier to win going through the front door – anyway, it's the way Kilkenny do it.

On the other hand, Justin didn't have the options he might have had if he'd treated the players differently. Brian Wall, our trump card back in 2004 from the bench, wasn't available, for instance.

We ended up playing Westmeath on a tight pitch in Mullingar in the qualifiers. We knew we were good enough to beat them, and it took us a while to get going, but we did it in the end. I ended up scoring 1–2 and should have got

5–2. That set us up for Tipperary in the All-Ireland quarter-final.

This time, we were ready. We had a full team, and everyone was healthy, myself and Mullane included. I had Hugh Moloney for company, but it was a better day for me than the Munster championship: I ended up with 1–5 and it was probably one of my best days ever in the county jersey.

I enjoyed scoring that goal in particular – I soloed in along the end line, the angle was fairly tight and Brendan Cummins came out of goal to cut the angle down further, but I was confident. At that stage Cummins must have been sick of seeing me. If I'm in that situation, bearing down on goal, I have it worked out in my mind, and if I can get one glimpse up at the goal then I'll know where I'll put the ball.

I study opposing goalkeepers, so I'll have a fair idea of what I think their weaknesses are. With Cummins, for instance, I'd notice the way he holds the hurley, left hand on top. That means it's an extra split-second's work for him to bring it across himself if I put it to the left side of his body, and that was what I did.

As soon as I hit the ball I knew it was going in. I just thought, *Forget about it, Brendan,* and put the ball across him and into the corner. We were up for that game. No matter who we were playing, we were determined that we weren't going to be known as a team that couldn't win in Croke Park. The leaders were the likes of Ken McGrath and Michael 'Brick' Walsh. I wouldn't class myself as a leader: I'd be quiet in the dressing room. At a certain point, too, I think you can have too many players talking and the team just gets distracted.

Some fellas are just too wound up before a game to take it all in. Mullane can be like a lunatic in the dressing room. His two legs are usually red from lashing himself on the thighs with the hurley, and he flakes himself across the body with it. That's his approach; that's what gets him ready for the game.

Brick is an awesome man in the dressing room. I couldn't talk highly enough of him; at half-time against Tipp he came in and told us that Paul Kelly had told him to 'Fuck off back to Waterford, ye farmer.' Brick was like a madman after that and he geed us up with it. He's a quiet man but he drove us on in the dressing room with it. (Of course, the thing is that Kelly was right: Brick comes from a farming background.) I often thought since that Brick should come into the dressing room at half-time in every game with some kind of insult from the opposition.

I tacked on a few points in the second half. I felt good – the team was right, the goal had settled me, and I felt I had the measure of the Tipp defenders. It was sweet to win one in Croke Park. Tipp came with a late run, but we felt we'd hold them out, and we did.

To win a game in Croke Park was a good day's work, particularly when it was Tipp. That was doubly true for the Waterford lads in Carrick-on-Suir, where the two counties meet. We saw a lot of happy Waterford lads from Carrick after that game, lads who were looking forward to Monday morning and getting a rise out of the neighbours from Tipp.

We were well set up for the semi-final against Cork. The thing was, though, I'd say Cork preferred playing us because we'd play hurling with them and keep it open – it wouldn't become as much of a physical battle as you'd get with Tipperary, say.

They came with a game plan, though. I noticed that Seán Óg was paying particular attention to me in the game and wasn't looking to burst upfield as much or to play his own game. I thought he was playing a different game and that he was nervous as a result. At one stage early on he tried a short line-ball back to Dónal Óg and I cut out the pass. I tried to chip Dónal Óg from a tight angle but it just happened to go over for a point.

With Seán Óg clearly focused on marking me out of it, Justin put me in on Diarmuid O'Sullivan for a while but we just didn't fire up front the way we should have. It was always enjoyable playing against Sully. He'd be good to chat to you; he'd be trying to take your mind off the game – to distract you, pure and simple.

Flynn was the same, always getting into his marker's head by talking to him. Himself and Sully had some conversations, both of them trying to distract each other: even with a big crowd, if you were jogging past them for a puck-out you could hear them yapping away.

Mullane would be good for a chat too, and you'd hear Sully shout at him to get into his head: 'Well, John, how's things today?'

Mullane would be cute enough, though – usually he wouldn't answer him unless he'd got a score: 'Well, Sully, how're ye going on?'

Sully would talk away to me as well – 'Take it easy on me now, Shan, it's hard going today,' all that kind of stuff.

I paid no attention. He'd be putting you off and then, when the ball landed, he'd lift you out of it and put the ball a hundred yards back down the field. Flynn was worse: he'd talk to the defender, get a score, then come back and talk to the defender again. Tormenting him.

Dónal Óg was noisy enough as well, but that was more about organizing the defence than distracting the opposition. He'd be sweeping behind the backs, out around the 21 when the ball was at the other end, and he'd be talking to them all the time. 'Tight there, Sully . . . tight there, Ogie, Ronan . . . concentrate, John . . .'

The funny thing is, you can hear the lads talking in Croke Park. Unless it's an All-Ireland final there's a bit of an echo in Croke Park because it's usually not full. It's a different story in Thurles or Páirc Uí Chaoimh: you'd be half deaf from the crowd and you wouldn't hear someone roaring at you from ten yards away. You'd just see their lips moving.

Back to the match: when Eoin got the goal for us just after half-time, I thought, *This is our day*.

We were in control with a few minutes left and Cork brought on a sub. I was thinking, *Who the hell is this guy Cathal Naughton? I never heard of him*. But he had a point scored straight away, then Deane gave him a lovely pass for a goal: 1–1 scored in a couple of minutes.

We just couldn't close the game out. If we hadn't conceded that goal we'd have made it to the All-Ireland final, but . . .

There was a chance late on, of course. We were a point down when Tony Browne was fouled in the middle of the field. Ken McGrath took the free, went for it, and it just came up short. I wasn't far away from it as it dropped in. Standing on the edge of the square, I was just a few inches away when I swung the hurley, but Dónal Óg batted it away down the end line and the game was over seconds later.

Close margins. If the ball had carried a foot higher it was a point and a draw; a foot lower and I might have had a touch for a goal and the victory.

When the final whistle went I looked back down the field through the rain, and I saw that Ken had gone down on his knees after taking the free. He knew it was over.

I won my second All-Star and we had another great night in the City West. It carried on to the following day. The Waterford Supporters Club in Dublin put us up in the hotel and took care of us for the day. Ann Condon was heavily involved in this. She is one of Waterford's greatest supporters. Any day, any game, she is there.

Towards the end of 2006 Dónal O'Grady's name was being mentioned as a possible replacement for Justin. A few of the lads spoke of him as a possibility, and then the rumour gained ground in Waterford, though eventually nothing came of it.

There were reasons for the dissatisfaction with Justin, principally a few of his selection decisions that year, which had put some of the players off, and they felt that a new approach might be good. It wasn't a serious heave against Justin, and any dissatisfaction didn't last too long, particularly when the county board gave him another year.

When Justin eventually left there was no shortage of people saying he'd stayed too long, and citing 2006 as the year he should have gone, but they missed one crucial fact about that year. There's no point in getting rid of a manager unless you have the right man lined up to replace him. The board backed him at that time, but there were a couple of little warning signs. Losing the likes of Brian Wall – and Brendan Landers, going back a couple of years – was something we couldn't afford. Other panellists were as dissatisfied as I'd been in 2002 and 2003: they felt they were getting nowhere.

Fellas wanted a bit of variety in training as well, but Justin always went back to the same schedule, starting off without the ball in January. We'd taken a lesson or two on board along the way. At that stage we had gloves that we'd bring along to the early sessions, just to save our hands from the blisters. Justin mightn't have been learning much more about us, but we knew what to expect from him.

It was hardly a surprise that we were considering Cork candidates again: I always felt Cork had good operators on the sideline, Dónal O'Grady being the obvious one (despite the slip I mentioned back in 2004). I've met him a few times at GPA awards and so on, and he'd always make very pertinent remarks – 'I notice you're coming infield more looking for the ball, Dan,' or 'You've improved your striking off your left: you must have been working on that over the winter.' What I like about him is that it's all hurling. When he's analysing games on TG4 or RTÉ, it's all about the game and the tactics, not players' personalities, unlike a few I could mention.

John Allen is the same – a very nice guy; John, Shane (John's son), Eddie O'Donnell and myself went out one evening for dinner and had a great night. He's a very good manager as well.

Of course, another Cork manager was a hero of mine as a young lad. I've met Jimmy Barry-Murphy a few times and he's a sound man. When I started on the Waterford team he was in charge of the Rebels but as a kid he was my idol. He could play any sport and could do anything with a hurley. We'd often meet him if we went out for a night to the dog track to Cork, and he'd always have a tip for a dog for us.

The Cork manager I knew best after Justin was Gerald McCarthy, of course, whose time with Cork came to an end after a big strike with the players, who didn't get on with him. I can only speak from our experience of the man: we found him outstanding. He brought Waterford up in the world big-time, and put down the foundations for Justin to work with.

When he went back as Cork manager I don't know if he had the respect of the players from day one, though they were all hugging him the day they beat Galway up in Thurles in the summer of 2008. By that Christmas they were all at each other's throats. Odd the difference a few months can make.

7 June 2010: Semple Stadium, Munster Semi-final

It's tricky, trying to get ready for the Clare game. It's on a Bank Holiday Monday, so it's not the usual Sunday routine. I head to the gym on the Saturday just to kill the time and probably do too much, but I'm just trying to put the hours away.

On the bus to Thurles that Monday morning Davy plays this DVD to get us going, and guess who figures on the film? Me in 2007, scoring goals for fun.

I enjoy watching it to an extent, but there is a bit of pressure as well, the lads nudging me and saying, 'That was some goal, Dan.' From my perspective I am starting a game after not getting a start in games the previous year, so I feel I have enough on my plate, but Davy slips over to me afterwards and says he thinks it will be good for me. Fair enough.

I'm conscious of the small crowd in Semple Stadium for the game; it's very noticeable immediately when we come out. If it was on a Sunday, there'd have been a far bigger attendance, but Bank Holiday Monday, fellas out the night before, sick with the drink . . . they're not going to head to Thurles to watch a game.

Our approach is a careful plan that Davy has worked out,

which can be reduced to one sentence: hit everything high into Dan so he can hang on to it until he gets support.

However, there's one small problem. Eoin is named at corner-forward but is told to play as an extra half-forward, while the other corner-forward is Mullane, who roams all over the field anyway.

As a result, I spend the game on my own in the full-forward line, with the nearest players fifty yards away; when I win the ball, though Davy says I can have a shot if I think it's on, in my head I feel he wants me to involve the other players so I feel I have to lay it off, but the lads outside wouldn't get near enough for a pass if they jumped into a taxi on the half-way line.

Frustrating? Stop. I have young Dillon of Clare climbing all over me when I have the ball and I'm under instructions not to go for my own score – the first ball I get I could put over with my eyes closed, but I hang on to it instead and we get nothing out of it.

The plan puts pressure on the lads outside to play the ball in high, as they're coached to let the ball off like that only if they're under severe pressure: look at the likes of Tommy Walsh – he'll only hit high ball if he's bottled up by two or three opponents.

It's no good expecting Mullane to play as an ordinary corner-forward, hanging near the square for the break, and it's no good expecting Eoin to be able to fly in for my passes, fast as he is. The logic of having one of the best forwards in the country far away from goal, rather than near the danger area, baffles me. At one stage Eoin ends up hitting the ball from half-back.

I felt positive about the outcome all through – that we were always going to beat Clare, even if we were four points down at half-time. Give them a few years and they'll be a great team but I thought our work rate was exceptional that day.

We need to start getting goals, though. We manage twenty-two points, which is good scoring, but we'll need goals, and with the plan we're playing to, we're not going to get them.

I have one chance in the second half, a sniff of a goal, and if I'd relaxed a small bit I'd have scored it, but I am conscious of the pressure – and I miss. That's the difference. In 2007 it was all on instinct.

I'm not surprised to be taken off, as Shane Walsh was going well in training, but I think a lot of the ball coming into the full-forward is mediocre at best. You look at Cork – Dónal Óg Cusack can put the ball in your pocket from 70 yards, while Gardiner is the best striker of the ball in the game. I was delighted for Dec Pender who came on and got three points.

I have worked hard and Davy tells me five scores came off my play after the game, but it's no consolation. It's hard to change your game like that because it's alien to players – if you've scored a lot of goals in the championship then you're not going to be as happy laying off the ball by order of the manager. That's not the same thing as popping the ball to a lad in a better position, which is something I've always done: I'm talking about getting specific instructions to win the ball and lay it off – even though he'd told me I could go for my own score, I felt he wanted me to involve the other forwards and lay the ball off to them.

Still, it's a job well done. We have a chat about going out for a drink, and though Davy can be very anti-beer for a former publican, he tells us to go out. We all stay together that night and go out in Dungarvan. Great craic. Now for the Munster final.

And Cork.

15

The year 2007 was a good one for me: highlights from start to finish. It began well and never really let up from there. We went to Spain for a warm-weather camp and came back flying fit.

The first most people heard of those camps was probably back in 2002, when Armagh went to Spain to train in May and had people laughing at them when they came back. No one was laughing a few months later when they won the All-Ireland football title. That success meant that every county in Ireland felt they needed to go to warm-weather training camps as well, and a lot have gone. It doesn't always work. Some counties clearly saw it as a new version of the Nutron diet, the wonder gimmick that would put you over the top and into the All-Ireland; other times you'd hear the odd yarn about camps that go a bit . . . off-message, as it were, but from my point of view the Waterford camps were usually very good. We got to train as professionals for a few days – focusing on the training sessions, recovery, tactics, with no distractions. If you committed to it you got a fair dividend.

I felt fantastic after the camp – I really saw the difference in my fitness and in my outlook. My attitude was changing towards training as I got older anyway; I knew I had to put in the work. That's not to say I skived off in earlier years: I did what everybody else was doing, but you realize eventually that that's not enough. You've got to train to be able to train, if you like. I remember a Tipperary hurler of the sixties saying that, and he was right. What you do in team sessions is just the topping-up, getting familiar with your teammates and the way they play. If you haven't the slog done on your own you won't get it done with the team.

For instance, I could go to the gym and meet my best pal, but I won't even speak to him while I'm there. I'm there for a reason: I'm in the zone and I'm there to work, pure and simple. After the session, fine, I'll talk away to him, but not while I have work to do.

The hard graft that nobody thinks about when they see me bounce out of the tunnel in Semple Stadium: it means doing an hour's circuit when I'd rather be at home playing with Chloe or doing a couple of hours' overtime for a family holiday.

When I say doing an hour, I mean it. I'm not talking about a few stretches on the multi-gym, then a look at Sky Sports News on the television in the gym or a smoothie in the car home to make me feel good about myself. It's a hard circuit with big weights, dreamed up by Gerry Fitzpatrick to make us suffer, not to pump our biceps to make this year's T-shirt look good.

It's serious. It's work.

*

We had a decent run in the league in 2007 on the back of the fitness we'd built, and we made it to the semi-final stages. We took on Cork and the day went well for me. Why wouldn't it?

It was late in the game when I picked up the ball near the Cork end line; I had no support and no real angle for a shot, so I drove it across the square and hoped for the best – and it shot into the net off Sully. Own goal.

The look on his face was worth four points, never mind the goal.

I know him well – why wouldn't I after the number of battles we've had? Most of the time on the field Sully would try to talk to me, to get me to answer him back while the game was on; he was trying to get inside my head.

The understanding he had with Dónal Óg behind him was unbelievable. If a ball went over our heads towards goal, he'd just hold me out. And I mean hold me – the hurley wrapped around me like a vice. I'm not a small man, but trying to get past Sully was like climbing over a tank. He was a diamond for Cork at full-back and if we had had him in the full-back line, I think we would have won one or two All-Irelands. I've known the man behind him since our underage days as well. As a result of that I've never had a fear of taking on Dónal Óg. I scored three goals against him in a Harty Cup final up in Fermoy, and a hat-trick like that buys you a lot of confidence.

But he's definitely one of the most improved goalkeepers around. When he first came into senior inter-county hurling he was inclined to make one or two mistakes in a game. That made his backs a little nervous and gave confidence to you if you were a forward – take the goal he let in against us in 2002 as an example. But he worked on his game, to his credit, and he became one of the best goalkeepers in Ireland. It was easier for Dónal Óg with Sully in front of him as well – they're two good pals and clubmates and they've always understood each other's play.

I'd love to have Dónal Óg pucking the ball out to me, certainly; he'd be a great man to have in goal back the field, because he'd put the ball into your pocket, he's so accurate. That doesn't mean I didn't enjoy scoring goals against him, but whenever Waterford were playing Cork, we always had the courtesy to shake each other's hands afterwards.

I didn't read his book – his sexuality and his private life are his own business, and I respect that totally.

As for his clubmate, Sully was a great man to rouse the Cork crowd. He loved coming out with the ball and meeting fellas with a shoulder, driving them back or lifting them out of it. The Cork crowd would roar and that would drive all of their players on. That was Sully for you.

When I was on him, he had his hands full. That famous picture says it all, the one of the two of us on our hunkers – which was during the league semi-final in Thurles in 2007, incidentally, not the All-Ireland quarter-final game in Croke Park, as a lot of people think.

People still ask me what I said to him, or what he said to me, and to the best of my recollection it was something pretty basic.

'I'm fucked, Sully.'

'If you're fucked, I'm fucked myself, Dan.'

Not exactly Oscar-winning dialogue, but that was all we were able for.

There's a bond between players from other teams, as well as between teammates. On the day of a game, you'd be ready to kill them to get over the line, but when you meet them at functions or even bump into them on the street, it's a totally different scenario.

Diarmuid O'Sullivan even had the courtesy to ring my father – he didn't have my number – to wish us the best of luck for the 2008 All-Ireland final, saying he hoped we'd win it. A tough full-back and a tough customer, but a guy I have a lot of time for.

Sully's own goal got us to the final, where we beat Kilkenny in a tight game – two points was the difference at the final whistle.

People have forgotten that league final. We haven't. It was a national title, and we've won few enough of them. If you want to know what it meant to Kilkenny to lose, you only had to see their faces: they were like thunder at the final whistle.

I didn't have a great day in the final myself, though, and I told Justin afterwards that I was disappointed, but he said, 'Dan, your goal got us to the final.'

Brick Walsh was captain that year. When he'd come in with us in 2004 he was a raw young lad, a footballer really, but Justin put huge work into improving him, and he did well with tough assignments – centre-forward, midfield, centre-back.

Nowadays he's a mainstay of the team. You'd hear lads

say, 'He's not a stylish hurler,' but he's a great man to catch the ball, and he's intelligent with it – that flick away with the hurley to pass it. He's also the only man you could imagine getting drunk on a glass of Coke, but that's another story.

That was the year Tipperary and Limerick had three great games in the Munster championship semi-final – two of them draws – before Limerick got through, but we had our eye on the other side of the draw.

It was also the year of 'Semplegate', when Cork and Clare had a brawl on the pitch before their Munster championship game. I watched that game on the television, and you didn't have to be psychic to see there was going to be an issue when Clare and Cork came out at the same time. People might wonder why they couldn't just let each other past, but that's easier said than done – you spend eight months obsessing about this crowd you're going to war with, you're running alongside them unexpectedly, someone lashes out . . .

The Munster Council would be well aware of that. How could they let two teams out together? They ended up flaking each other and grappling on the floor, though it was only for a few seconds and none of them was hurt.

Of course there was uproar after it, but that's because it was a terrible game when they got down to actually playing it – if it had been a cracker you'd never have heard anything. Cork won, but Seán Óg, Sully and Dónal Óg were suspended, as were some Clare players, but we were facing Cork, so we were interested in what kind of team they'd have. Then they appealed it, and the whole appeals process – rigmarole, more like – began and everybody was in limbo, waiting.

While we were waiting to play them in the Munster semi-final, this was going on in the background. It wasn't a distraction, particularly. I'd have preferred the three Cork lads to be playing: first, I didn't agree with their suspension for nothing more than handbags, as everyone described it at the time, but also we wouldn't have known the lads who were coming in. Plus, we'd have been expected to beat them because they were under strength. As far as our preparation went, it would have been better to have Sully, Dónal Óg and Seán Óg there, because mentally our lads would have known they were in for a tough battle.

The appeals process dragged out through the weeks leading up to our game with them. Eventually their last appeal was turned down by the Disputes Resolution Authority on the Saturday before the game – less than twenty-four hours before the throw-in. It had to be a huge distraction for them, knowing that half their first-choice defence was either going to be (a) suspended and ineligible to play, or (b) not suspended but exhausted and unable to play. That was particularly important for the goalkeeping position, as it meant that whoever they were bringing in would have less than twenty-four hours' notice. According to the rumours doing the rounds in Cork – and beyond – Dónal Óg would play if the suspension was lifted the night before the final.

On the day our focus was good. We didn't notice, for instance, when the three lads suspended on foot of

'Semplegate' came out on to the sideline, though people told us afterwards that they'd been given a huge roar by the Cork supporters when Gerald embraced them.

We could tell Cork were under strength. Their full-back line wasn't as intimidating a proposition without Sully, and they wouldn't have been as confident either without Dónal Óg behind it. Out the field they were missing Seán Óg, but people forget that John Gardiner had had to appeal his suspension and give evidence and so on, so he had to be fairly distracted as well.

That's all in retrospect, of course. At the time we were just focused on ourselves and getting the job done as well as we could. And it went pretty well, as we got four goals in the first half.

I scored one of them when Seamus Prendergast broke through. I was on his shoulder roaring for the pass, and for a second I thought he wasn't going to give it, but he waited and waited, and by the time he got buried by a shoulder charge from one of the Cork backs, he'd just popped the ball to me and I blasted it in. Goal.

The second came closer to half-time. We'd scored two more – through a Flynn penalty and Mullane – when an attack of ours was broken up by Ronan Curran on the 21-metre line. The ball rebounded back to me, and I had more time than you'd expect in a Munster championship game so I looked up.

I thought I'd place it. The goalkeeper, Anthony Nash, had come to his near post, leaving a huge amount of space on his left-hand side. I placed it, and it worked out well, the ball flying into the top right-hand corner.

You have to take a different approach with different 'keepers. With Dónal Óg it used to be power, but he has improved hugely. Some of them fancy their chances against a forward in different circumstances, but they all like the ball at shoulder height. You have to work them, so you keep the shot low, even if it's a smaller 'keeper, like Davy Fitzgerald.

It was funny the way the ball fell for me for my second goal – rebounding off Curran. Whenever Justin thought the game was tight, he thought Curran could be taken and he'd put me in on him. He often said Curran didn't like marking big men, and I felt he was right, especially in 2007. We had a few run-ins, the two of us – a few thumps thrown in matches, nothing too serious. He'd be chatty enough: he said to me that day, 'You won't get much today, Dan.'

I said, 'We'll see, Ronan.'

I got the two goals off him, but I never laughed at him or took the piss out of him. I had too much respect for him to do that.

I was happy with my afternoon's work. Two goals against Cork in a Munster semi-final? I'd take that any time.

Sully was a loss for Cork that day, and you could tell from the goals we got – they came from going down the centre, where he'd normally block them off. Justin had us well prepared that day, too: he'd have known well who Cork would have full-back and he told us we'd get goals.

I ended with 2–1 and we scored five goals in all, so he wasn't wrong.

We had Limerick in the Munster final. They'd come through

a rough examination themselves with those three games to get over Tipperary.

Players often say they'd prefer the practice of more games to training. It's the old attitude, which says, 'That championship game is worth three weeks' training to us.' It must have been an ancient cliché a hundred years ago. It's true enough, but only to the extent that those games don't take over your life totally, which was what happened to Limerick and Tipperary in 2007.

It destroyed Tipperary's season, as they never really got over the fact that they'd had chances to beat Limerick and hadn't taken them, and it finished Babs Keating and his management team as well – they were gone by the end of the season.

The three games destroyed Limerick's Munster championship hopes as well. They came out of them exhausted in the short term, but they'd learned a lot about their team. That would help them in the medium term, but we didn't care about that. We had a Munster final on our hands.

We were fresher than Limerick – and more experienced. I was on Mark Foley in the Munster final – a fine hurler and a good striker, but not the tightest marker in the world. He liked to play his own game at wing-back, which is something a wing-forward would be delighted with. He won the first ball that came down between us, and I fouled him coming out. When he won the free he turned around to the crowd as if to say, 'We're on top here', and the Limerick supporters roared back at him.

I've grabbed the crest on my jersey often enough over the years, so I wouldn't be criticizing any fella for showing his emotions on the field. Each to his own.

Foley playing to the supporters didn't bother me on the day, and that's experience. In 2007 I had almost ten years' experience under my belt. It had been that long since I'd first played in a Munster final. No matter what roar my marker got from the crowd after winning a ball, it wouldn't bother me in the slightest. I knew my chances would come. I wasn't going to roll into a ball because of a bit of noise.

I didn't open my mouth to him, just did my best to mark him and get my chances. I had a good understanding with Tony Browne back the field, and he set me up for three points that day. There wasn't as much roaring from the Limerick crowd when they went over.

I remember everything about that game because it's a day that will never leave me. For my first goal, Flynn took a shot, and the 'keeper, Brian Murray, saved it, but I was on the edge of the square and pulled: goal.

Limerick came back and came back, but we didn't panic. We were focused, we knew they'd have their chances, and we knew we'd have ours.

For my second, Brick Walsh won the ball and got it across the field. I flicked it past Brian Lucey and got round him, but I made a hames of the shot, no question about that. Still, the intention was the thing – I did what I'd always been taught: I hit the ball into the ground and it skidded off the wet grass and in under Murray for another goal.

For the third goal, I was in acres of space inside the cover. I don't know who was marking me at that stage and I'd say they didn't know themselves. Even in a Munster final, with months of planning, someone can draw a blank and just forget his job, who he's marking, and that's what happened for me when Seamus Prendergast popped in a pass to me, all alone twenty metres from the Killinan End goal.

Think of being in that position for a second: all alone in a Munster final, so close to the opposition 'keeper you can literally see the whites of his eyes, knowing that if you just keep the ball away from him when you shoot you'll have bagged a Munster final hat-trick, the kind of feat you would have been embarrassed even to dream of as a child. All you have to do is keep the ball away from him.

I went for the crowd-pleaser, aimed for the top corner – and it flew in. Beautiful.

Eoin McGrath came running over when the third one went in and hugged me, but I just shouted at him, 'Run out there to wing-forward and cover for me. I'm shagged.'

It was phenomenal. That was the only day I ever walked up the steps in Thurles, up to where they present the cup. Usually I'd head over to say hello to Chloe and the family after a game, and just go straight to the dressing room, but it was different that day. I wanted to drink it in, every moment of the win. To savour it. Justin was delighted for me, and I was delighted to get the scores for him. I don't think there's many get 3–3 in a Munster final.

We were expecting Tipp in the All-Ireland quarter-final; they seemed to be going nowhere with Babs, and they were lined up to play Cork in the qualifiers, which were different that year: the teams played three games, with the top two going through to the quarter-finals. Cork looked streets ahead of Tipp, and the talk was that Eoin Kelly was injured, or that Babs was going to drop him. We thought Cork would destroy them with the three Semplegate lads back in harness.

I was at James 'Joxer' O'Connor's wedding the day they played each other, in the Clonea Strand Hotel – drinking water the whole day, obviously. The time when I'd join in for the toast and lash into the beer the week before an All-Ireland quarter-final was long gone. Andy Moloney and Fergal Hartley, who were also there, spent the afternoon drinking away and telling me how sweet the beer tasted.

We were sitting down for the wedding dinner when some lad came in and said Tipp had beaten Cork. That was a bit of a shock. And a bit of a readjustment.

Left: Colette and me with Chloe at her First Communion.

Below: With the family after receiving the Park Hotel Sports Star of the Year award in 2007. (*Left to right*: Maurice, Pauline, Brian, Colette, myself, Mary, Sharon and James.)

Above: My parents came to watch me play in Croke Park in the 2008 All-Ireland final.

Below: Chloe's the apple of my eye and has been a great supporter at matches.

Above: I've been criticized for celebrating goals by kissing the crest, but for me it's a matter of respect for the team.

Below: 'If you don't know me, don't judge me.'

Above: A moment I'll always regret, when I refused to shake Justin's hand after being taken off in the 2008 Munster game against Clare.

Below: Eoin Kelly has always been a good friend, as well as being my first cousin.

Above: Myself and John Mullane in training with new manager Davy Fitzgerald.

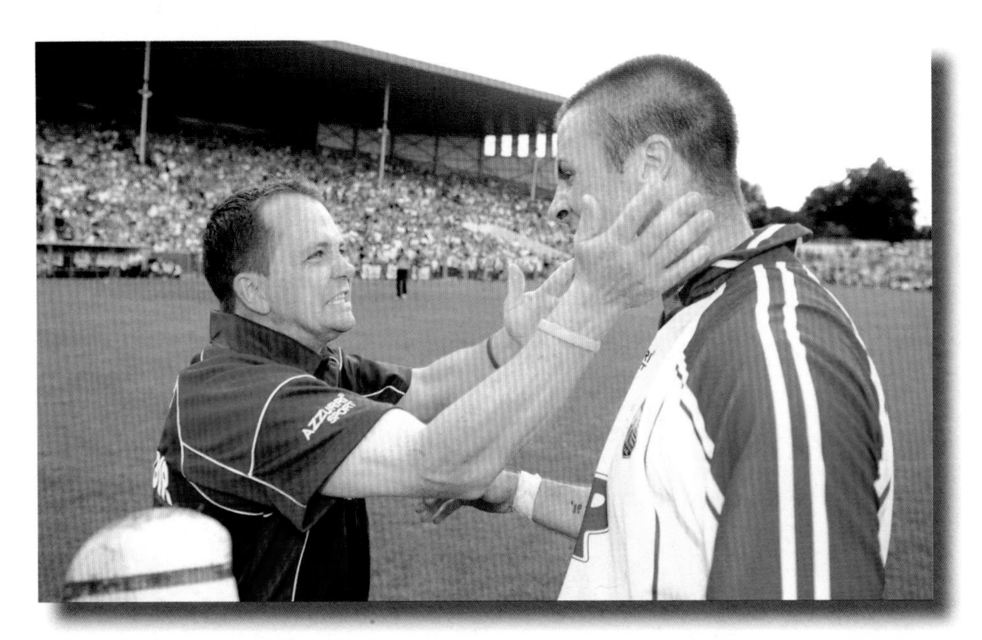

Above: Enjoying the win with Davy after we beat Wexford in the All-Ireland quarter-final in 2008 on one of our better days.

Below: Trying to get past Brendan Cummins in goal for Tipperary in the All-Ireland semi-final, with Paul Curran hot on my heels.

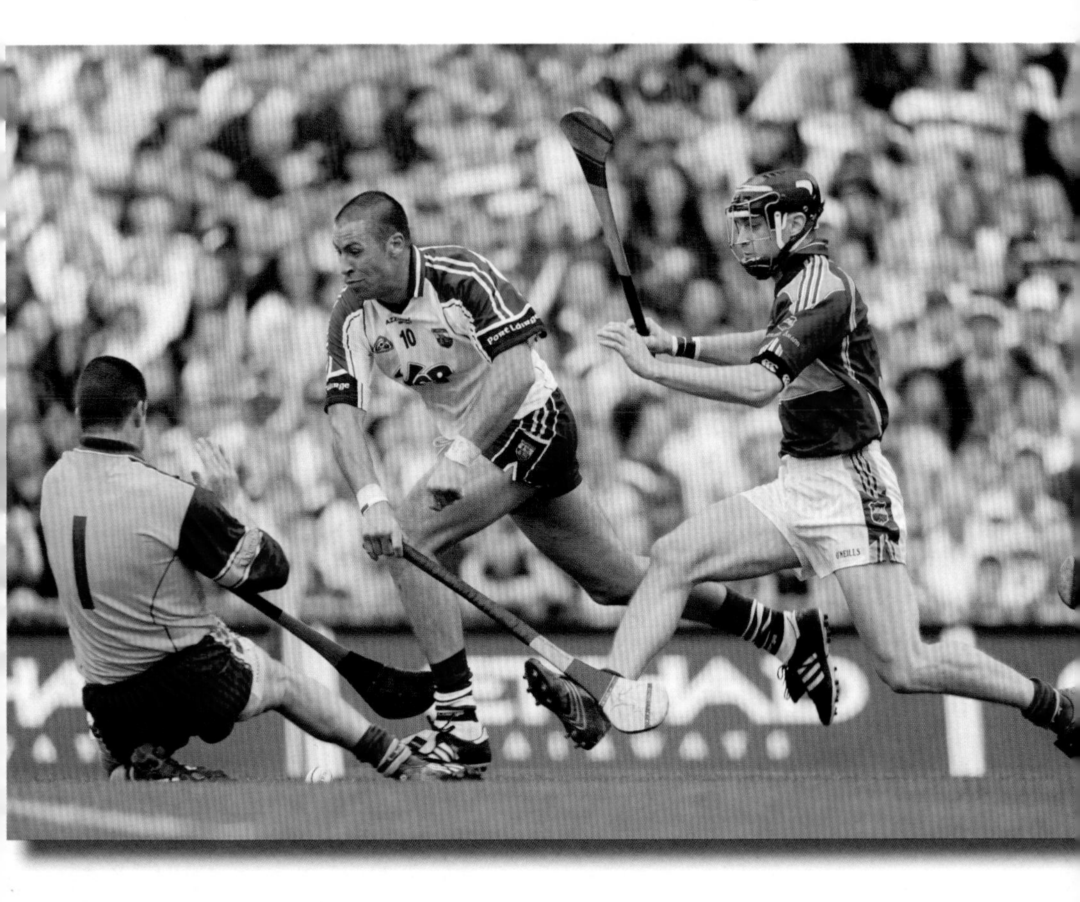

Kilkenny were all over us in the 2008 final – literally in the case of Noel Hickey and JJ Delaney.

Above: My goal in extra time secured the win in the 2010 Munster final replay against Cork, with Maurice watching and learning!

Below: Celebrating that goal!

A treasured moment of victory after the 2010 Munster final.

16

The first match against Cork we were in trouble. They were well up for it, and it was obvious that they felt they'd have done better against us in Munster with the three lads who'd been suspended after Semplegate. They had us under pressure for most of the game, and Kieran Murphy and Neil Ronan were doing a lot of damage.

We needed a goal: we were three points down and Cork were looking like they were going to stretch out their lead.

The ball came in over the Cork backs from Tony Browne, I came on to it, and it sat up beautifully for me. I managed to lose Ronan Curran and it came right up into my hand.

I had one place to aim for, and that was at Dónal Óg's hurleys, which were stacked in the far corner of the goal, on his good side. I picked them out. I was used to picking a target and aiming at it; I often spent hours in the field at home hanging a tyre in the goal, or a jumper, and aiming for that, and this was an example of that practice coming good. I hit that target.

There were photographs of me afterwards, which showed a Cork hurley flying through the air from behind – obviously one of their backs was frustrated – and you'd think it was going to fly across my hurley as it arrived, but that's an illusion.

I wasn't even aware of the hurley: trying to get a goal against a 'keeper like Dónal Óg, you wouldn't have much time for other distractions. Dónal Óg dived full length and he nearly got to it, but it went in.

Stephen Molumphy was absolutely crucial to us that day. He mightn't have many scores to his name after a game, but he's a great man if you're an accurate forward: if he goes in to win the ball with two defenders, then you know to stand off, because he'll win it and pop it out to you to take your score.

Molumphy – or the Lieutenant, as we call him – was a serious addition to the Waterford team. In 2007, he had a huge influence on my performances – he set up at least five of the eight goals I got in that year's championship, I'd say. (Not that we don't have our run-ins at club level: he's from our local rivals over the road, Ballyduff, who wouldn't be too fond of Lismore.)

Cork went ahead, but we rallied. With time almost up we were one point down when Eoin McGrath picked up the ball in oceans of space about forty yards from the Cork goal. He could have dropped it, picked it up, dropped it again and picked it up again before getting tackled, and all he had to do was pop the ball over the bar for an equalizer.

Eoin didn't do that, though: he put his head down and went for goal when there was a point on offer that would draw the game – and the little so-and-so never got a goal in his life, I'd say. (I'm joking. He was right to go for it: if you've a goal chance you should always go for it, and we needed a goal to win it.)

McGrath took a decent enough shot and Dónal Óg saved it but deflected it across the square, where I was hanging around. Unfortunately, I was too quick in after it to follow it up. If I'd just stood where I was it would have rolled right out to me.

Close? I looked down and could make out the O'Neills logo written on it as it rolled out underneath me. Then Flynn made contact: it was heading goalwards but it hit Sully's backside and Dónal Óg threw himself on top of it.

Flynn was standing over him with the hurley, ready to pull, roaring at Sully, 'Get your fat arse out of the way,' but the whistle went. Dónal Óg had covered the ball, though, and it was a free. The referee got that right. There were other instances during the game when he threw the ball in for lads sitting on it, and while Brian Gavin wouldn't be the most popular of referees at the best of times – we had our own run-ins with him – he got that call right. Cork complained a lot afterwards, and they might have had a bit of a point when it came to the consistency, but they should also answer one simple question: if it had been the other way around, would they have expected to get a free?

Those games were wicked fast and I'd wonder if Gavin was able to keep up, but no matter what the Cork lads might say, he was right to give us the free in.

Eoin tapped the ball over the bar for a point. Draw.

After the game we were shaking hands when I came up against Gerald, who was managing Cork. 'Well done, Dan,' he said, but his teeth were gritted and the look in his eyes suggested he may have been thinking, *Thanks a lot, Dan, after all I did for you.*

I was about to remind him about the time he'd told us he wouldn't coach against us, but I decided not to. In the end I just said, 'Thanks, Gerald,' and headed into the dressing room.

As I was leaving the stadium a radio journalist stopped me for a comment about the last free, and asked me what had happened.

I told him the truth – that the ball had hit Sullivan's fat arse – and thought no more about it. Years later I still hear them playing that bit of tape on the same radio station!

In the replay we won well. I scored two goals. The first one came in the twentieth minute, when I got a hand-pass from Molumphy and buried it.

For the second goal, the ball broke over the Cork defence and I hit a ground stroke and the ball went into the bottom right-hand corner. I had a bit of room, so I got in a beautiful stroke off my weak side; Diarmuid O'Sullivan had given me a bit of space and I just turned and struck it.

After I took the shot, I registered a couple of impressions of the scene, like snapshots. First I saw Dónal Óg lying on his face. Then I caught a sight of the ball in the net – it had flown right into the corner. As I went back out, Flynn said to me, 'Come on, you're the man!'

I ended up with 2–1 that day, and we got through.

Then we had Limerick in the All-Ireland semi-final. Just like Cork, they were a team we'd already played but, because of the draw against Cork, this time we were the ones playing three weeks in a row.

We felt it, too. Usually you've got a couple of weeks

between games, so you can do a bit of physical work to keep yourself ticking over after you've played a match. Then, in the week or so leading up to the next outing, you sharpen up your touch.

In 2007 we were going from game to game, with no real chance to work on either fitness or touch. You might ask if three games in three weeks would take that much out of players physically, and strictly speaking we'd be fit enough for them.

But mentally it takes a toll. By the time it comes to the third game, when that's in the melting-pot and you need to work on instinct, to drive yourself on beyond the point of tiredness, you don't have those vital few per cent that you need. It's not the physical exertion of seventy minutes the previous two weekends: it's more to do with the talk about the match everywhere you go, when you turn on the television, listening on the radio in the truck. The game seems to be everywhere, from the moment you wake up until you go to bed that evening.

All we could do week on week was a bit of recovery in the pool. Before we knew it we were in the hotel for a big game again. There's no let-up. No respite. That's where the tiredness comes in – it feels as though it's been going on for months, with no break.

I think if Cork had beaten us they would have refused to play three weeks in a row. I'd say the legendary Cork County Board secretary Frank Murphy would have found some kind of rule that would have meant playing on the following Saturday. Not that we weren't playing well. After the games against Cork, people were saying, 'How will Limerick beat Waterford? They're flying altogether.'

But they did. The likes of Gary Kirby for Limerick would have been cute enough to have on the sideline. Everyone remembers Richie Bennis was the Limerick manager, and his big hug for Babs after one of their games in the Munster championship, but Kirby was the hurling brain, as far as I was concerned. I'm sure he'd have noticed things to improve on – and stuff we were weak on. We'd have been a bit flat anyway, but they approached the game very well.

I played well that day. I got four points and I made Molumphy's goal. I'd skimmed the post with another shot and could have had a goal but the ball just ran away from me at the vital moment. We were ten points down when I got away from Stephen Lucey and put the ball across for Molumphy's goal, for instance, and that brought us back into it.

Lucey tore my jersey to pieces that day, and I showed it to the umpires but they didn't want to know. It's a funny thing: fellas would say to me, 'Would you not take a dive?' – but I couldn't. For one thing it's not my style, but there's also a more sensible reason. If you're six foot three, you're not going to win frees that easily if you start flopping around on the ground. I think that, subconsciously, referees expect you to be able to mind yourself when you're that size.

This was the game where Justin was beginning to lose his way a little when it came to the team, I think. He took off Flynn and Mullane when we were trying to win the game and threw on Shane Walsh, who was only a young lad. No disrespect to Shane and the other subs, but that was a mistake. You don't take two match-winners off in a game you're trying to win. They mightn't have been having their greatest games, and you might take off one of them, but Flynn would be dangerous if we got a free within thirty yards of goal. With him gone, we didn't have that option even if we'd won a free. As it was, the biggest cheer of the day came when the two boys were taken off.

Still, we were coming back into the game. Tony Browne got a massive point and we attacked again, but Shane missed a pick-up, Limerick launched it downfield and Brian Begley caught it and was floored: penalty. Andrew O'Shaughnessy took the penalty and buried it. He was awesome that day. We'd minded him well in the Munster final but he cut loose in the semi and tore us to pieces.

After the game Richie Bennis was all over the television and the radio saying, 'We got five goals and Dan got none' . . . That really annoyed me. I shook his hand after the match. I didn't know he'd be raving about that stuff later. I got four points, won a few frees and set up a goal. If Limerick had had me, they'd have won a few games too. Richie was probably delighted with the win and I wouldn't hold it against him long-term, but it was annoying at the time.

The Waterford lads ended up with a league medal and a Munster medal that year. It was Limerick who ended up with nothing.

I think we would have had a decent chance in 2007 against Kilkenny if we'd reached the final that year. We had momentum, the team was a year younger than it would be in 2008, we'd have had another couple of weeks off to recharge . . . I was very disappointed the Waterford County

Board didn't dig their heels in and stop playing the third week in a row.

I'm not saying we'd have won in 2007 – but it would have been great preparation for 2008. Now, you could make the argument that Kilkenny would have been a year younger as well, but they weren't at the awesome peak they reached in 2008. If we'd made the 2007 final and got back there the following year we'd have been in a far better position, but it wasn't to be.

The year didn't end for me there. Tommy Walsh in particular had a good year for Kilkenny, and they'd won the All-Ireland. Usually the Hurler of the Year award would end up with one of the All-Ireland champions, but I felt I had a chance. I'd had a good season. I'd scored 8–12 without taking frees, which had to count for something.

When it was announced that I had won the Hurler of the Year award, they opened bottles of champagne in Lismore. We had a night in the club, and having my clubmates around me that night was fantastic. A lot of the lads on the county panel came out to Lismore that night, too, which was great: I'd made a point of accepting the awards I got that year on behalf of the whole team.

It was great to win the GPA award too, because the prize was a car. A trophy is great, but I have to give credit to the GPA: an Opel Astra is phenomenal.

I'm a strong supporter of the GPA. Dessie Farrell and the lads have done great work and they try to sort out jobs for hurlers in Cavan and other places, where they train as hard as us but don't get the recognition.

The GPA are so well organized and they put in an enormous amount of work. They make a presentation if you win a Player of the Month award, with a cheque for a thousand euro. With respect, the GAA would give you nothing. There wouldn't be a need for the GPA if the GAA looked after its players, and I hope the GPA keeps going. I don't agree with pay for play, but players could do with good mileage, good gear and a nice holiday after the year they put down.

Some county boards can get players jobs, though in Waterford they don't seem to be able to do that. I don't know why; you'd imagine that with the profile the team has had in the last ten or so years it would have been easier, particularly during the boom. The GPA are trying to do that, though. In Cork, for instance, Paudie Kissane is looking after coaching in football, and Martin Coleman and Brian Murphy are doing the same in hurling.

The county board in Waterford should appoint players who aren't working – and with the recession biting so deeply now, there's no shortage of those – as county hurling coaches. It wouldn't cost the earth to give a couple of those players vans and gear and let them loose, one in the east and one in the west of Waterford. The kids would love it.

The people they have coaching nowadays in Waterford, whether through the various FÁS schemes or whatever, are doing their best but we have inter-county hurlers out of work who could do that job brilliantly. I've gone along to some coaching days where kids are holding the hurley the wrong way. I have nothing against the lads doing the coaching now, but if you wanted to train as an electrician you'd go to an electrician to learn.

I would have been interested in that myself: when the glass factory was closing I did a course in coaching. I went for a job and didn't get it but I rolled in with Comeragh Oil instead.

17

There were plenty of whisperings against Justin towards the end of 2007. There had been the substitutions of Flynn and Mullane against Limerick; the fact that many of the non-starting players weren't getting any serious attention; and boredom, plain and simple. Some of the players just got bored listening to him. The information was still good, but by 2006 or 2007 we were sick of listening to the same voice.

To some extent that exists in every panel at all times. Despite what you hear to the contrary, you can be sure there are lads in Kilkenny who aren't happy sitting on the bench; lads who'd be happier if there was someone in charge who'd give them a game. That's only natural. You put in the same effort as everyone else, you make the same sacrifices, and even if you're not starting, you feel you're as good a player as anyone else. Dissatisfaction with the manager is part of every team sport.

But this was different. The substitutions of Flynn and Mullane the previous year against Limerick confirmed what some of us felt: that Justin wasn't handling games that well. Although I'd got over his very distant manner once I began to get a start on the team, other lads on the fringes of the team found him remote. And the training, while it had been fresh when he'd come in, was the same thing over and over again. By 2008 it was our seventh year of it.

You might say that Man United always listen to Alex Ferguson – but they're consistently successful. They'll put up with anything if they're winning medals. With Justin, over the last couple of years we'd been getting tired of doing the same thing. He'd been very good for us, and for Waterford hurling. We'd been knocking on the door, but he'd helped to unlock it, and most of us had three Munster medals in our back pockets as a result of his work, not to mention All-Star awards. We owed Justin a huge debt, and that's not an empty tribute. But after nearly seven years, the end was in sight.

It wasn't that we simply decided one day that it wasn't working with Justin. Our management team didn't have the right dynamic – Seamie Hannon had been there at the start with Justin and was there at the finish with him, and many of us felt he was Justin's right-hand man. I respected him when he'd talk at match previews on Thursday nights before big games, when we'd be sizing up the opposition, and the players would listen to him going through the following weekend's opponents.

But we felt that the mix among the selectors was wrong – if the manager has men with him they're there for their opinions, not just to agree with him. Some of us felt that if Justin was picking the team, Seamie would agree with him, which only reinforced Justin's attitudes about players. You can't have anarchy among the lads on the line, arguing about every little switch and change, but they shouldn't agree with everything the manager says either.

When we had good selectors, we couldn't hold on to them. Kevin Ryan from Mount Sion was a very good selector with Justin, but he didn't stay involved that long. Kevin was good with players – he had a fair knack for telling lads where they were going wrong and what they could do to improve, and the proof of that was the success he had later on when he took over Carlow, and with the clubs he trained.

The ideal would have been to have the continuity there was in other counties, where a guy comes in as a selector and learns the ropes before he becomes the manager. That way, when he becomes an inter-county manager he's not starting from scratch and making his mistakes in the course of a championship season.

Kevin could have benefited from that approach but it didn't happen.

I was in the spotlight a lot that winter of 2007 and the following spring. Justin was probably not too happy with me having a higher profile after winning the Hurler of the Year award, which meant I was presenting medals, opening shops and that kind of craic, but I did plenty of it. It was a fantastic time for me, meeting people I'd never have come across otherwise.

Guinness came up with a game – Guinness Cubed – which involved hurling in an enclosed space, big enough for just half a dozen players. I spent the day of the launch with Stephen Hunt, the soccer player. We ended up heading to Flannery's in Dublin, in his Porsche. Good craic, but we didn't have a drink, believe it or not. He was a great guy and a Waterford lad – we could have done with him as a roving corner-forward – and he was the only fella fit enough to play the Guinness Cubed game. Myself, Seán Óg Ó hAilpín and Gordon D'Arcy were all down to go in and have a go, but at the time we were all injured. It had nothing to do with the Guinness Cubed game, but it probably wasn't the best advertisement you could have had for it – everyone endorsing it was crocked, though they hadn't been injured playing the game itself.

I had the privilege of meeting another Waterford great, John O'Shea, who plays for Man United. Myself, Henry Shefflin and Kieran O'Connor (who got the match tickets) saw John play in a Man United v. AC Milan game. It was a great evening, especially when John made a huge effort to meet us in the hotel that night. We really appreciated the effort.

I also met Brian O'Driscoll around that time at the Texaco Sportstars of the Year awards, and it just goes to show how wrong you can be about people. I'm interested enough in rugby, and I'd follow the Irish team and Munster in particular. I have great time for them, how they've overcome so many disappointments to come through as champions. (There's a fairly obvious lesson for us in Waterford there.) However, I wouldn't take as much interest in Leinster.

I had always marked O'Driscoll down as a typical Dublin-4 guy, someone who'd have no interest in GAA and who'd certainly have no idea who some Waterford hurler might be. Not a bit of it. I met him at the function and he couldn't have been sounder. He showed a fierce interest and chatted away about the hurling season, and from then on I took a keen interest in how he got on. He's a warrior. Texaco Awards are fantastic for the simple reason you get to meet great people from all other sports.

It didn't all go smoothly. I won the Park Hotel Sports Star of the Year, which is the top sports award in Waterford. It wasn't an occasion for sticking to the tea and toast.

We had a game in the Waterford Crystal League the following day in Fraher Field against Limerick Institute of Technology, and I was picked to play full-forward. Jackie Tyrrell of Kilkenny was full-back, marking a man who'd had a fair rake of vodka and Lucozade the night before at the ceremony. I didn't want to be there at all and couldn't wait for the game to be over – to go on the piss again with the lads, pure and simple.

Jackie didn't know that, obviously, and decided to test my ribs with a few digs here and there early on. No harm in that, and on any other occasion I'd have ignored it. Not that day, however. It was the first and last time I ever really lost the head and hit someone. Jackie Tyrrell isn't someone who'd take that and not hit back, and I ended up getting and giving a few digs. The fight, short as it was, was my fault. It was the most serious run-in I've ever had on the field. I'd say a few lads I played with – and against – are probably reading that and thinking, *He calls that a run-in?* But it was for me. I felt bad afterwards, so I went looking for Jackie after the game to say sorry. I didn't find him, but I did bump into Cyril Farrell, who was managing LIT at the time, and asked him to pass on my apologies.

But I don't know what Justin was thinking, putting me on that day. He knew I'd won the award, that it meant a lot to me and that I would have been celebrating. I could have approached him and said I couldn't play, or didn't want to, but I didn't. I thought he'd let me off, given it was a relatively unimportant game, but he didn't, so I ended up fairly pissed off. Along with collecting a few bruises.

Then again, it was a fair indication of how things would go for Waterford that year.

18

The atmosphere wasn't good in 2008. The training was very poor – the enthusiasm wasn't the same as it had been, but the regime was exactly the same, and lads were sick of it.

The management team didn't seem to be working either. For instance, we felt that Gerry Fitzpatrick didn't seem to be getting enough time with the team at training sessions to put his programme into effect properly.

It's fair to say that a lot of the players were unhappy even before that season got well and truly going with the league. Justin became a focal point for a lot of that unhappiness. Part of it was personality-driven – the intensity that had been so impressive back in Davitts in 2002 was beginning to wear thin. There was no let-up in his attitude: it was hurling, hurling, hurling the whole time, and fellas weren't inclined to give him the benefit of the doubt any more.

The fact that Justin didn't come across as particularly warm didn't help. He didn't seem to show much interest in lads' lives away from the training ground or match days, which was fair enough for a while but eventually began to grate on us.

What fecked the whole thing up, though, was the trip to Spain for training.

I was injured at the time. I'd hurt my knee in a club game – I went through the opposition defence with the ball, my leg jerked underneath me and I knew it was hurt. Dr Tadhg O'Sullivan was worried I'd torn my cruciate and sent me for a scan. While it wasn't that bad an injury, it still set me back.

But I wasn't fully fit anyway. To be honest, I was enjoying myself a bit too much – blackguarding – and was banking on getting myself fit as the year went on, but the injury set me back. That all added up. The training wasn't as fun, so I'd think, *I'll turn it on in the match*. But that's not how it works. You have to put it in when you're training to be able to turn it on.

Because of Guinness Cubed, I was late flying out to Spain to join the lads, and it wasn't the same. We'd had a terrific training camp in 2007, and got to the All-Ireland semi-final on the back of it, but this didn't compare. Some of the other lads were unhappy I didn't go out with them, and some players were unhappy with the way the whole set-up was going. In retrospect the elements were all there for a confrontation. While most lads trained hard, not everyone gave the same level of commitment to the camp as in previous years – put it that way.

It was against that kind of background that Justin said in Spain that if anyone had any suggestions about training they should make them. The players had plenty of suggestions they wanted to make. They wanted training changed – and fast. Brick Walsh and Ken McGrath went to Justin and said more intensity was needed, more variety in the drills and so on. They had a sheet of paper with ten items on it, but Justin didn't take the suggestions well and obviously took the criticism personally, when that wasn't what was meant. That was the finish of Justin, in my opinion.

He didn't seem willing to change. If he'd freshened training up, he might have survived, but it was the first time that the players had told him what they wanted. It was nothing to do with the fact that we were away. As I said, we'd been away in 2007 and it was fantastic – the weights we lifted in the morning, the speed of the hurling in the afternoon: it improved us hugely.

But in 2008 it was different. I couldn't train because of my knee and a couple of the lads were saying, 'You were okay to go to the Guinness Cubed thing but you can't train.' It was a distraction, but who'd refuse a few euro like that if it was there to be made for the family?

Justin didn't take those suggestions on board and at the end of it we weren't even training. We ended up playing a game of soccer on the last day out in the resort and Justin just walked past. I was standing in goal and saw him pass.

It spoke volumes, though, that the lads had more fun playing a soccer game than training for the championship.

When we got home things didn't improve, even though we beat Kilkenny in Walsh Park the weekend after. We had a training session before the Munster quarter-final against Clare, and Justin made Bryan Phelan take twenty penalties, with the forwards following them in. Bryan Phelan had never taken a penalty in his life; if Justin had had Paul Flynn taking them, fair enough – but Bryan wasn't going to be taking them in a championship game.

Did Justin get tired of us or did we get tired of him? A bit of both, probably. We definitely did the county board's job for them. In 2007 they should have said, 'Thanks for everything you've done, Justin, but it's time to part company.' He'd done unbelievable things for Waterford hurling, he'd brought us all on, but the romance was definitely over.

Eoin was dropped for the championship game against Clare. Ken was injured. I was injured as well and shouldn't have played, but I did. I felt I couldn't *not* play – I'd had a good season in 2007 and I owed it to everyone to line out, even though I was well off my best.

As I said earlier, on the day the preparation wasn't good. We were out in the blazing sun in a hayfield before the game, hitting a few balls around, grass up to our shins, instead of going to a club ground.

Then the Garda escort broke down on the way to the game. While we were on the bus Justin had a CD he wanted to us to listen to – some kind of inspirational thing. If he'd come up with that the previous season, or a few months beforehand, we'd have bought into it, but to bring it in like that . . . It smelt of desperation. It was all wrong.

We had a few lads who did themselves justice that day. Not a lot. Mullane played well, Tony and Brick were very good, but Clare won. I had a nightmare day. I was beaten off the field by Conor Plunkett all through, and I wasn't surprised to be taken off. I could have got the old call ashore ten minutes beforehand.

As I came off the field, Justin stuck his hand out to shake, and, as I said earlier, it was the biggest mistake of my life that

I didn't take it. The crowd in the covered stand saw it and they reacted immediately with a roar. The Clare crowd were in top form already, as their team was coasting to a decent win, and I suppose the Waterford crowd were in the mood for a distraction.

I parked myself with the other subs and tried to blot out the abuse. My daughter wasn't so lucky: Chloe was there with her aunt, my sister Pauline, who asked a couple of ignoramuses next to them to stop using bad language about her father. Some hope. They eventually had to move seats because it was too upsetting for Chloe to have to listen to those supporters; I'd love the chance for a chat with them myself some day.

I didn't know then that that moment marked the beginning of me getting some amount of shit. If I'd even said to him after the match, 'Justin, I'm sorry I didn't shake your hand,' things might have gone differently, but I didn't.

The dressing room was in an awful state. It wasn't like a normal defeat. We've lost plenty of big games, and we've lost plenty of close games, but there's some kind of consolation when you've given it everything and just come up short. Everybody shares the pain: players, officials and management.

This was different. It wasn't that we'd seen it coming, because we always go out positive for a Munster championship game, but it was no surprise to lose, and certainly no surprise to lose the way we did. We could tell how bad things were from the atmosphere in the dressing room after the game. The unease was palpable. The players weren't speaking, they weren't engaging with the management at all, and when we got on the bus, the majority of us went to the back. The talk was simple enough: he's got to go. It was that quick.

Because Clare had beaten us fairly well there weren't a whole lot of match highlights to pick out for *The Sunday Game* that night, so there was a lot of round-the-houses talk about trouble in the Waterford camp, with yours truly held up as the prime exhibit. Peter Finnerty in particular made a big deal over me not shaking hands with Justin when I was taken off, and I wouldn't have much time for him over that. Fair enough, he's on the television to give his opinion, and that was something people were talking about – but he didn't have a notion about what was going on within the camp.

The following morning the picture was all over the newspapers, and people were jumping to some fairly wild conclusions, saying the Waterford performance was all Shanahan's fault. I hadn't intended to do what I did coming off the field but people had seen it; what I didn't realize at the time was that some photographer had decided to track me with his camera and got the photograph that was worth a thousand words. I'd have got fairly sick of seeing that picture over the next few days if I hadn't been distracted.

On Monday – the day after the Clare match – I got a text from one of the other lads to come to the Majestic Hotel in Tramore that night for a players' meeting. It wasn't hard to guess what the main topic for discussion would be.

It was hot and heavy, an emotional meeting – and no

wonder. We said we were there to work everything out, but it was clear from early on in the meeting that most of the players were unhappy with Justin as a manager and wanted him to go.

Tony Browne said we had to be careful, as this was a man's livelihood we were talking about – he spoke very well all night, in fact, saying that if we did something we'd have to do it together.

We stayed there until two in the morning thrashing it out, and I had my say along with everyone else. The big difference, though, as I told the lads, was that I was the focal point for all the speculation. 'Lads, ye don't understand,' I said. 'I'm getting the brunt of this thing because I didn't shake the man's hand. The shit I'm getting is unbelievable, and if Justin goes I'll be the one getting the blame.'

Someone said then that if Justin went we'd all be taking the blame, but I disagreed: I said I wouldn't be taking any of the blame because I had no problem saying what way I'd vote.

Although we agreed to abide by the decision of the majority, it wasn't as though Justin had no support in the meeting. There were seven players voted for him to stay, and I could name them. I was one of the seven who voted for Justin to stay because I didn't agree with changing horses in midstream. That was my attitude. I didn't think we'd get anyone better in the middle of June, and asked what the point was in changing if we had no hope of getting anyone better at that stage of the season.

But the majority of the senior players wanted Justin out, and some of the speakers were very strong in wanting him to go, and the majority ruled. That was the way we'd agreed it. A lot of the younger lads wanted him to go because they felt he didn't know them and that they weren't getting a chance to win a place on the team.

After it got into the media that we'd met up, the county board weighed in. We told them we weren't willing to play under Justin as manager, so it might have become a situation like Cork if it had developed, but it never did. The board told us they'd be willing to back us, which was fair enough, though then again, we were the ones getting criticized, not them.

And we were getting some stick. I got a call from the county board one evening and the chairman, Pat Flynn, said 'We've a letter here addressed to you but I'd advise you not to open it. I'll open it.' I told him to go ahead, and when he did, he said, 'I'm not showing you what's in this. It's disgusting.' A letter with a Kildare postmark.

I was also getting texts that were unbelievable. I still have them: they were just pure abuse. 'You're the man to blame'; 'I know what you're up to'; and those are the repeatable ones.

A letter like the one Pat Flynn opened meant nothing to me – but getting those texts was different. I'd be at home with Colette and Chloe and I'd get one, which is a fair invasion of privacy, and I had to check my phone in case it was work-related.

I ended up going to the guards, and the sergeant I spoke to asked if I wanted anything done. I said I just wanted to cover myself, but through another channel I eventually tracked down the address of the person sending them, and then, of course, I knew who it was. I wasn't the only one getting that kind of rubbish – Brick was getting abusive texts as well as Jim Dee.

I felt bad enough as it was without that. I'd started off poorly with Justin, when I felt he didn't rate me, but we'd come on, and he'd been good for me, improving my skills, while I'd been good for him, getting the goals to win matches.

That photograph . . . fair dues to the photographer for getting it – it was a brilliant picture for him to get – but I'm sure as long as I'm playing, whenever we play Limerick, or any team Justin manages, that picture will be in the paper.

Justin was gone within a couple of days. The county board rowed in with us straight away, unlike other counties where the boards had taken the manager's side. He didn't hang around. I read in the *Examiner* that he was gone and that was that.

We wanted Nicky Cashin and Michael Ryan to stay on as selectors, but they were gone too. Gerry Fitzpatrick stayed on, which was good: we'd been in touch with him and wanted him to stay because he was such a good trainer. So did Peter 'Chunky' Kirwan as physio. The great Jim Dee also stayed on as team secretary.

All that time, just before Justin went and for a while afterwards, we were listening to so-called experts on *The Sunday Game* and elsewhere talking about player power in Waterford. They didn't know what was going on at training and so on – all you'd hear was people saying, 'By all accounts this, by all accounts that.' I know they're expected to give their opinions, but they'd want to get their facts right first. Either they didn't know what they were talking about, in which case they were wrong to speculate, or else they had an idea what was going on but didn't come out and say it, which is just as wrong in my book.

We had decided not to talk about the Justin situation to the media, which wasn't easy. I remember going to an Adidas press call not long after he'd left, and trying to avoid the questions. I felt, rightly or wrongly, that I was a focus for a lot of the discussions about Justin. For instance, I went up to Clare to watch the Waterford footballers play a match, and I had a coat on and a baseball cap jammed well down over my face – yet a photographer still found me and took a picture of me. No escape. Maybe they thought I was going around the country avoiding handshakes with everyone I met.

I've never really spoken about what happened that time, and this is a relief to me now, to get it off my chest. I've never met Justin since. I still have his number on my phone and I'd love to ring him and apologize, but I know he wouldn't have it. I'd love to be able to make my peace with Justin, but I can't. That's a regret.

Davy Fitzgerald wasn't our first choice. We were thinking of Donal O'Grady, Nicky English, Liam Griffin, Anthony Daly or John McIntyre. The usual suspects that come up, if you like, whenever there's a high-profile hurling manager job on offer, but I was proved right. Because it was the middle of the season the county board – which had set out to find a replacement – had difficulty finding someone who'd take the job on.

There was also the perception people had of us – that we'd shafted Justin and were somehow undisciplined and ungrateful. For a couple of days we were wondering if we'd get anybody.

For me, Nicky English would have been a great appointment. He was the best manager Tipperary had had in my time, I thought. He struck the right balance: he was passionate enough to lead them but he was also scientific and modern in his approach. I'd met him after winning the Granville Sportstar of the Year Award in Waterford in 2007; he came down and we got on great. (I told him I'd forgiven him for not giving me an autograph in 1989!)

I had great time for him as a player. He was a great finisher and shipped a lot of punishment at a time when there was very little video evidence used to protect forwards. Nicky would get absolutely leathered every time he had the ball, and he'd often come off the field after games with bandages around the head.

But the talk was that he'd be going to Dublin, the job Anthony Daly took on. Not even the fact that he's married to a Waterford woman could get Nicky on our side!

Anthony Daly would also have been a huge bonus. We felt he had a soft spot for us. I remember in 2008 when we played Wexford up in Thurles and I scored 1–1. Coming off the field that day I looked up and there he was in the stand, working for RTÉ, and giving me the old thumbs-up.

But we all saw Davy on *The Sunday Game* when he was asked about it, and though he foxed a bit, you could tell he was interested. Even the look on his face gave him away.

We had no say in his appointment. The board chose him,

not the players. Pat Flynn came back to us and said, 'He's the best we can get,' and we accepted that.

Which meant that four years after I'd scored three goals against him, Davy Fitzgerald was now my manager.

11 July 2010: Semple Stadium, Munster Final

The Tuesday after the Clare game Davy tells me that I probably won't be playing against Cork.

That's disappointing to hear, two weeks before the game itself – you think, What's the point in training if you know you don't have a chance of making the team?

I have a fair idea I won't play; a forward's job is to score and I didn't score against Clare, but there's no great incentive to train hard if the manager tells you that you probably won't start.

At our next training session we play A v. B games and I do well on Liam Lawlor, so it's disappointing when I know it's not going to happen, but I keep the head down and work.

Before the game I wish every player the best; Bernard Dunne the boxer is there with us for moral support and he is brilliant.

The first half of the Munster final is tit for tat, seven points to six. Liam Lawlor has to go off because he's on a second yellow card, and Jamie Nagle comes in. Cork get two second-half goals and go ahead, but the lads never give up, and Eoin Kelly gets one of the greatest goals I've ever seen in Thurles.

Davy brings three of us on at that stage, with a point in it.

I'm at full-forward and Mullane, who's flying, goes to the corner, which doesn't suit him.

We get an injury-time free when we're three points down. Eoin lines it up and I notice that everyone is lining up on his right, so I line up on his left. I've been here before: in 2005 against Cork *I took the same angle and goaled when Flynn's shot was saved. I know the scenario.*

Eoin's shot is good, hard and low, but it's saved and it rebounds to the right, where the crowd is – and Tony Browne buries it. A great player and a great finish. Draw.

19

I'll give you an idea of my dealings with Davy Fitzgerald before he became Waterford manager. We were both on an All-Star trip back in 2005, and I was playing on the team against him, stuck in at corner-forward.

These All-Star trips are exactly as you'd imagine – a chance to go on the lash for a few days in a foreign country with the lads you usually play against, so the games wouldn't be on the cutting edge of competitive, put it that way.

This particular game had barely been going two minutes when my marker said to me, 'Do me one favour and take one shot on the 'keeper, will you?' Davy was the 'keeper. The first ball came down between us and the man marking me nearly let me have it, then made a half-tackle to let me through on goal. I let fly from close range at Davy and buried it.

Not really the best foundation for a good relationship with your new manager.

Davy made one great move when he brought in Maurice

Geary and Peter Queally as selectors. I've known Maurice all my life: he taught me in school so I knew he was a fantastic coach, no matter what the level of the game. When he came in with Davy he proved it, too. He ran tremendous drills for the backs and was a huge asset. A great man to read the game.

There was another angle to Maurice's involvement – he was from Ballyduff, the same club as Seamie Hannon, Justin's selector, so I'm sure he'd have taken some flak within his own club over coming in under those circumstances, but he was brave enough for it.

Peter had been a player with Waterford when I started back in 1996, and was hugely committed in training always. Not the most skilful player, as he'd admit, but he gave a great example to everyone, and he was the same as a selector.

Not all of us got off to a great start with the new man. I had a run-in with Davy the first evening he came down to Walsh Park (we had a disagreement about the team's tactics, which I'll get to later), but to be fair to him, his training drills were good. We were under pressure to do well after the departure of Justin, and Davy's sessions were fresh and interesting. Even the different voices at training improved things.

For myself, I wasn't as fit as I could have been but I got in shape eventually, even though I could see by the tactics Davy had in mind that they weren't going to suit me. The previous year I'd scored goals for fun by drifting in behind the full-back line – keeping the opposition defence guessing as to where I'd be. But Davy wanted us away from goal – out the field, out the field, out the field, as he said – and that took me miles away from the danger area.

On top of that I had a bad sciatic nerve problem. I had pains all up the backs of my legs and in my back.

So: I was upset over the Justin issue, which was still rumbling on in Waterford, even though Davy had come in; I was generally unfit and had a specific injury; and I knew the new man's approach wouldn't suit me. Tough times.

In the few months he had with us in 2008, Davy was very good. He focused on ball-work in training and was totally professional: we rolled in for a session one night and he had T-shirts and gear waiting for us in the dressing room, instead of fellas wearing a mix of everything – club tops, county jerseys, T-shirts, soccer tops. This was a step forward. It meant there were fewer distractions when it came to training; all you had to bring was your hurley and boots, and a good attitude.

Davy also brought in a sports psychologist, though I wouldn't really agree with that. I think it's a manager's job to get the players' heads right. He should know how to get them ready for a game, and the only way to do that is to know all your players inside out. Granted, that takes time, which was a luxury Davy didn't have in 2008.

We all had to meet the psychologist, and when I had a session with him he wanted to know if I had any personal problems going on. I felt that was a bit close to the bone. My attitude was that there was only one fella who could deal with the hate mail and texts I was getting and that was me.

I could understand Davy feeling he had to try different things; he had to hit the ground running. He brought in stats men, which I wouldn't agree with – who knows better than yourself if you're winning the ball from puck-outs or not? – but he also brought in people like Bertie Sherlock as a trainer, fellas who were very positive; he brought in a goalkeeping coach as well, so we had not only different voices at training but different ideas. That freshened the whole thing up after years of listening to just one voice.

I was bad in 2008, to be honest. As I've said, I was unfit at the start of the year, and after the Justin thing my head wasn't right. It would have been hard to keep the right attitude with the abusive texts I was getting, which continued all that summer, but eventually, in the Park Hotel in Dungarvan, I confronted the person who was sending them and asked what they were doing. The answer I got was that one of my teammates was sending those texts. As if anyone would believe that.

What made 2008 worse was that 2007 had gone so well. The year before, almost every ball I got ended up in the back of the net. In 2008 I couldn't seem to get a break, no matter which way I turned.

When we eventually got back on the road, we had Offaly in the qualifiers, and got over them.

Against Wexford it went a bit better for me: I got 1–1, but it could have ended for us there and then in Thurles. We gave away a penalty in the last minute when we were two points up and Damien Fitzhenry came up from his own goal to take it. Clearly a 'keeper doesn't run the length of the field to pop it over the bar, and he went for it. He struck the ball perfectly too, but it shot just over the bar rather than underneath. We were through to an All-Ireland semi-final by a matter of inches. People can remember Mullane hugging Davy on the ground. Given the year we'd had, that was no wonder.

Part of the reason we hadn't played well against Wexford and Offaly, which nobody really picked up on, was that we were still getting used to Davy's tactics. Justin hadn't been inclined to get bogged down in the small print when it came to strategy: he'd tell you to go out and do what you think. But that had gone, and Davy's approach was totally different.

That different approach didn't suit me. My knee wasn't quite right, and I still had the sciatic nerve problem, so I wasn't confident about my fitness; that meant lads were ahead of me early in the season and I was struggling to get up to their level for the rest of the year.

On top of that Davy was on at me to come back out the field during games, the opposite of what I'd been doing for years under Justin – he wanted me protecting the mid-fielders and half-backs, while Justin had given me the freedom to ghost into the full-forward line whenever I felt it was the right option. I don't know if Davy's tactic was a throwback to his days with Clare, when they had stronger backs than they had forwards, but it made things harder for our forwards, certainly.

It was Ken McGrath who changed all of that for me. He could see I wasn't happy with the way things were going, and before the Wexford game, he said to me, 'Do your own thing. Don't mind coming back the field, just go out and do what you've always done.'

As a result I scored 1–1 against Wexford. People said I had a poor year but those were the scores that got us through to face Tipperary in the semi-final.

There was no fear of Tipp, even though the media had made their minds up that they were the only team in Ireland who were going to give Kilkenny a game – just as soon as they made it to the All-Ireland final.

On paper the odds might have favoured them but, to dust off that great GAA cliché, we were quietly confident, and with good reason. We might have struggled to get over Offaly and Wexford but we always knew we'd have one big game in us, and you don't get a half-hearted invitation to the All-Ireland final if you didn't play beautiful hurling along the way.

And Tipperary helped us as well. People probably don't realize that the factor which really swung the All-Ireland semi-final for us was that Tipp had had their hotel booked for the All-Ireland final long before they played us. That got to us immediately: it added fuel to the fire.

How Davy found out I don't know, but that's the GAA for you. There's so many people from so many different counties stuck in so many places that these things always get out. He made a big deal out of it – 'Look how little respect they have for us! They're taking us for granted,' and worse – and it worked. The minute he mentioned it, it got into people's heads and they were focused. It became the single thing we remembered.

On one level, it was understandable for Tipp to book that hotel: it's a big group of people, and if they'd left it until after the semi-final, they might have struggled to find a hotel for everybody. The question nobody thought of asking in our dressing room, of course, was an obvious one: what were *our* arrangements?

When Lismore played a county senior final against Ballygunner last year, we had a dinner booked in a hotel for the entire team. We drew the game, which meant we had more training and a replay to look forward to, but we still had to head off to the hotel and eat that dinner. You wouldn't knock much fun out of your beef or salmon in those circumstances, but what would you do if there was nothing booked and you won?

In that context, Tipp were just planning ahead, and looking back now, in the cold light of day, I know that's all there was to it. It wasn't disrespecting us. It wasn't such a big deal. But to a team preparing for an All-Ireland semi-final against them, it became a very big deal indeed because it suited us to feel insulted over the 'lack of respect' it showed.

Add in a couple of simple facts: we didn't fear them and we also played exceptional hurling on the day. It was close enough at the end, but we hit the ground running against a young Tipp side who were coming to terms with a long lay-off after the Munster final and looking to find their feet, most of them, in a big senior championship game in Croke Park.

Davy was a lucky manager, and that's not an insult. In Offaly and Wexford we had two grand stepping-stones before we played Tipp in the All-Ireland semi-final. Fair enough, it nearly went pear-shaped when Fitzhenry took the penalty, but it didn't, and we got everything right for Tipp.

We turned it around that day, and Davy was a huge part of that. He was very good in the dressing room. He gets very worked up before a game – I'd say most GAA fans with access to a computer have seen the clip that appeared on YouTube, with him roaring and shouting before a game, but for all our disagreements he was badly let down there, I thought. I felt it was wrong to put that on the Internet; the lad who did that broke a confidence and let Davy down – we've all said and done things behind closed doors we wouldn't be thrilled about seeing on the Internet. But it's fair to say that Davy tends to get very worked up in the dressing room before a match and he was pretty worked up the day we played Tipp.

We started well, that was the big thing. We were six points up before they got going, which was probably the result of having had a few games in recent weeks; we got into it immediately.

Unusually for us, we also showed a bit of cuteness. The best example of that was when Eoin Murphy went down after Lar Corbett caught him across the face. It slowed things and put pressure on them. Murph was injured – he got a couple of stitches on his chin after the game – but it didn't help Lar Corbett's cause when the man he'd hit looked half dead on the sideline, with Davy Fitz jumping up and down screaming blue murder at the referee from about two yards away.

Lar was booked for the challenge and I thought Tipp

made a bad mistake in leaving him on after that. He's not a dirty player by any means, but he was obviously rattled by the incident and the booking, and it distracted him for the rest of the match.

I didn't think the game went that well for me, but I won a few frees that Eoin Kelly pointed, and late on I managed to send in the ball that Eoin doubled on to get a save out of Brendan Cummins. When he reacted to the rebound quickest we had the goal that set us on our way.

Davy came up to me afterwards saying, 'You did well, you won a few frees, you set up the goal.' But he might as well have been talking double Dutch. When the final whistle blew we just looked around at each other. And then erupted.

We were in an All-Ireland final.

We didn't see eye to eye, myself and Davy, in 2008. I'd say he thought I was riding on my reputation a bit, after winning Hurler of the Year in 2007, that I was taking it easy by maybe pretending to be injured. There's no way I'd fake an injury, though – you never know when that kind of pretence could come back to haunt you. I had that sciatic nerve problem, but I suppose a manager who doesn't know you is going to be suspicious when it's not obvious that you're hurt, which is the case with most back problems.

Davy's pet tactic of withdrawing players back the field seemed a negative one to me. In my book, the forwards are there to get scores. But he made it clear he wanted Mullane and Kelly, speedsters, in the full-forward line with plenty of space around them to operate, and that meant keeping away from the full-forward line.

Davy was trying to bring in a Kilkenny tactic – or maybe the old Clare tactic – of protecting the defenders with a withdrawn half-forward line, but I just didn't have the fitness to play that game.

He talked to me one-on-one about our tactics, just as he had one-on-ones with other lads, but one thing that might have been an issue – which was never really addressed – was the bitter memory of the 1998 Munster final between ourselves and Clare, or even the 2004 championship game when we beat Clare handy. It was a topic nobody felt comfortable about bringing up properly.

Davy had played in both games, and while they were mentioned, it wasn't done in the right way. At times we'd be training in Walsh Park and someone would get a rise out of him, saying, 'Would you not go into goal and try to stop a few shots, Davy? Didn't Shanahan get three against you a few years ago?'

They were joking, but he didn't like it – that much was obvious.

The likes of Flynn, Bennett and Feeney from the '98 team left, though Tony Browne and Ken McGrath stayed on, and were well worth keeping.

However, Davy did try to play Ken at full-back, and I knew well Ken didn't want to play there. It was like Justin bringing Hartley back to play full-back in 2005 – if he'd brought him back to play centre-back, and maybe left Tom Feeney at full-back, we might have beaten Cork both days that year.

Taking Ken out of half-back was robbing Peter to pay Paul, though all the plans worked out, come the Tipp game. We were in an All-Ireland final, and Davy was entitled to say his tactics had got us there. But we got there with Ken playing centre-back; Davy had to move him there for the semi-final, and it paid off.

The new manager brought the preparation to a new level of professionalism. The board backed him when it came to resources, even when he brought in the psychologist – and that was a big difference from the previous man. Justin wouldn't have entertained any of that. He was the boss at training, and he said what was what; I think he might have seen anyone being brought in with a specific area of expertise as a threat to his position.

Davy, though, would bring lads down from Limerick Institute of Technology, fellas with different ideas, experts in mental preparation, to help us focus for the big games. One of them told me one night to take out my aggression and anger on a punchbag; he held it and I hit it. I could see what he was trying to do, I suppose, but I was struggling at a lot of the training sessions anyway, and because of that I'd be in bad form. You didn't have to be a psychologist to work that out. Or to hit a punchbag to know it.

Davy would never ask me directly about my humour: he'd ring one of the lads and ask, 'What's up with him?' instead of asking me straight out. If he had, I'd have levelled with him: the kind I am, if I was in bad form going to training I'd cheer up during the session after I'd hit a few good shots or whatever.

If Davy wanted to know why some lads were unhappy, he wouldn't have had too far to look. A couple of times, after I'd had a bad game, or training had gone against me, Davy mentioned All-Stars in the dressing room, stomping around and throwing the comments out. 'So-called All-Stars, Hurlers of the Year, who do ye think ye are?' It was that kind of thing. And then he was wondering why I'd be in bad form. That kind of talk wasn't going to put anyone in a good humour.

I kept the mouth shut and worked on.

Davy brought the preparation up a notch, but anyone would have got us to the All-Ireland semi-final that year, I think. We'd made the commitment to doing that. We had to do it. After Justin left we had to produce the goods; we'd made a rod for our own backs, and we knew it. People were surprised when Cork got to the All-Ireland final in 2003, having been on strike the previous winter. Now that we had been through a similar situation, I can well understand how that kind of thing can drive a team on.

Tipperary manager Liam Sheedy came in to us after the Tipp game and spoke from the heart. He's a genuine guy: he wished us well in the final and said he hoped we'd win.

We got crates of beer for the trip home, and we had some laughs on the way back to Waterford, but we had no idea what was waiting for us. The train driver let us know there were people in the station – and were there ever. It was a great scene, the crowds waiting for us. Of course, people had turned out for us before, after we'd won Munster championships, but this was unbelievable. We were applauded as we stepped off the train. There were people in white and blue all over the platform singing. We partied well that night and got up the next morning to get ready for an All-Ireland final.

20

The county just went cracked ahead of the 2008 All-Ireland final. It's as simple as that. Davy did his best to keep us out of the limelight and to keep the focus on the game, but it was an impossible situation. You can't stop people enjoying the build-up to a game, enjoying the anticipation, especially when it had been so long since Waterford were last in an All-Ireland final. They'd gone cracked, and they were entitled to be, after waiting nearly half a century.

But it's impossible for players to be shut away from that as well. In my job I'm going around talking to people all day, delivering oil. What was I going to say to them in those couple of weeks? 'Sorry now, I can't talk about the match because I want to stay focused. Would you ever just belt up about the match?' If I did that, they wouldn't be long getting the order somewhere else.

One of my orders is a delivery to Austin Flynn, who lives just outside Dungarvan. He was the Waterford full-back in 1959 – we could have done with him a few times in the last few years – so he understood the situation I was in. 'I'd love to see ye win it,' he'd say.

'We've been there too long altogether. Ye should take over.'

When he said that, I knew he meant it, too. Now, there's a couple of fellas from that 1959 team who would hate it; they'd cut us to pieces when they talk about us – 'They've no heart,' that kind of thing – but Austin would walk out to the truck with me and he'd always say to me, 'They're on about us too long. Go on now and win it.'

Tom Cheasty, one of Austin's teammates, said the same to me before he died. Tom was a legend in Waterford, a huge man who drove on that team, and when I used to meet him he'd shake my hand – one of his hands was bigger than my two – and say, 'Come on, it's time for ye to take over.'

The obsession with the final got into everything – where we were staying, what suits we would be wearing, when we were going up, what we would have for our dinner after the final, and that's without getting into lads talking about Kilkenny. Alex Ferguson would have found it hard to manage that situation.

The maddest evening of all was the open night we had in Dungarvan. That summed up how crazy it had become.

We had a training session that was to be open to the public, and it was mobbed: thousands turned up. How someone wasn't seriously hurt I don't know – every player clung up to the wire, trying to sign autographs, the crowd everywhere, small kids trying to get out of the way. Carnage.

It wasn't all hectic – my father met Diarmuid O'Sullivan, and Sully wished me all the best in the final: 'You've only one chance so make the most of it,' he said.

The training was good in the run-up to the final. Davy

brought in some different drills and had us taking a lot of long strikes, but I felt frustrated. After all the years, I wasn't right for the final. My fitness wasn't good, I wasn't happy with the tactics, and I wasn't right in myself. The time dragged as well. I thought the board might play club games to break it up, but those were all off so there'd be no distractions in the couple of weeks before the final. In retrospect a round of local games might have broken the tension. Then there was the manager's approach.

Davy had it in his head to target five lads on the Kilkenny team, to get into their heads. That made no sense to me, and that's not being wise after the event. You're going out to pick on lads with four or five All-Ireland medals at the time, remember. These are great players – you're not going to put them off with a shoulder or a dig; that's why they're great players.

Worse, he picked the likes of Eoin Murphy and Seamus Prendergast to get stuck into their opponents. The wrong men. There were players on our team who would have had no problem getting stuck into their marker – they'd have been getting stuck in, to put it mildly, as part of their normal approach – but not those lads. Having said that, if he'd told me to start a row with a Kilkenny player I'd have done it, but he didn't. That wasn't Eoin's or Seamus's natural game – but it was in their heads going out that it was something they had to do, and obviously it was a distraction.

That's not the right way to send a player out for his first All-Ireland final. We'd never done something like that before. It was alien to our players.

Apart from that, Davy had been very good in the build-up, but when he came up with that as the master plan in the week of the match I was worried.

We went up on the Saturday morning and stayed in the Marriott Hotel in Ashbourne, and they treated us like royalty. They were fantastic. But loads of Waterford people had booked in there as well, and we were meeting them in the hotel, all over the place, and there was no getting away from it – the talk about tickets, about history, about Kilkenny. No escape.

The experience of that weekend was a learning process for us. Kilkenny were going for three-in-a-row, and they'd hammered Limerick the year before.

I still maintain that if we'd won the previous year against Limerick in the All-Ireland semi-final it would have been terrific preparation for the 2008 final; we'd have learned an awful lot. As it was we had to pick it up as we went along that weekend.

I love chilling out in a hotel room. I'd have loved to be on my own, but I was in with Tom Feeney, a lovely fella and a great guy to room with. We relaxed on the Saturday evening, chatted away. Mullane came down for a chat.

I'd a fair amount to think about. When we'd been away on a training weekend Davy had come to my room to talk to me about JJ Delaney. 'He's there to be taken, Dan,' he was telling me. 'He's away down in Kilkenny, saying he's going to clean you out – "I marked Shanahan before, I'll do it again." He's there to be taken.'

That put me off – I had enough on my plate trying to get

myself right with an injury without him telling me stuff like that. Maybe he was trying to build me up, but it had the opposite effect.

On the morning of the game I felt the occasion all right. I don't often get nervous but there were some nerves that morning. An All-Ireland final. About ten of us went to mass. I always say a prayer before a game, and that day I figured there was no harm looking for a bit of extra help. Afterwards I just relaxed in the room until it was time to go to Croke Park.

I can tell you one thing: when you come out on to the pitch in Croke Park on the day of an All-Ireland final, you know it's a final. The sound tells you, for one thing: there's a difference between the sixty thousand people you'd get for a semi-final or maybe a Munster final and the eighty-two thousand at an All-Ireland final. It's phenomenal: it surrounds you and you can't hear a person screaming at you from ten yards away.

I looked up into the stands when we got out and I could see people in Waterford tops crying with the emotion of the thing. Old people. Children. That's about all you can do in the first twenty seconds or so: just look around and take it in. The first person I'd always look for is my father, then my family and friends – they've always been there, even when things were going against me. I was glad they were there that day after all those years.

We were tense enough in the warm-up. We had a slightly different warm-up routine for the final and fellas weren't used to it – we might have been better off jogging in to stick the ball over the bar; it would have been better for the confidence than getting jumbled up trying to rise the ball in groups.

It got worse in the pre-match parade when one of our lads dropped his hurley. I wouldn't blame him – we were all feeling the heat at that point, just waiting for the game to start.

Then Eoin Murphy hit Eddie Brennan at the start of the game and it was over. It was as if they thought, *This is the best they can do?* and went into overdrive. They just unloaded and destroyed us. We caught a great team on their best day.

From number one to thirty-one they clicked, and there was nothing we could do about it. Martin Comerford hit one wide for Kilkenny and was taken off. TJ Reid came on as a sub and got four points.

It was a horror show. Goals flying in. Points hammering over. At half-time we were in an awful state in the dressing room. The game was over. We knew it. We knew we hadn't turned up. Not one of us could say he'd played well.

Tony Browne stood up and said, 'Look, lads, we've come too far to let ourselves be done like this.' But it was too late. The dressing room was like a morgue.

Davy made a couple of changes, putting Ken McGrath up centre-forward. We had nothing to lose.

Dave Bennett came on for me with ten minutes left – and he got a point, so at least he scored in an All-Ireland final. I got nothing. I had two half-chances of goals – for one, I thought Michael Kavanagh fouled me. I shouted out at Barry

Kelly, the referee, 'Jesus, Barry, he's all over me,' and he just said, 'No, no,' and we played on. Barry's a good referee – his style is to let the game flow, which suits the way Kilkenny play – but I thought he got that wrong. I had the other half-chance in the second half, but that was it.

Then they brought on their sub 'keeper, James McGarry, for his last game. That showed us how much of a threat we were, when they could afford to change goalkeepers without affecting the result.

In the dressing room, we didn't know where to look. Nobody wanted to speak. We just wanted to get out of there and get to the bar. The fact that we lost so heavily wasn't the management's fault. It didn't help to take the approach we did, but it wasn't their fault that we lost the All-Ireland final like that. We were the men on the field.

We went up to the players' lounge, had a few drinks, then headed back to the Burlington and drank it out.

The following morning, Clinton, myself and a few of the others were up early. We bumped into Donal O'Grady in the lobby and he advised us to keep it together until we got back to Waterford, that there'd be kids at the homecoming and so on. 'Ye can cut loose then,' he said. 'That's what we did when we lost All-Irelands.'

'Yeah, Donal,' said Clinton. 'But ye never lost an All-Ireland like we did yesterday.'

Someone asked Clinton if it had been a long day for a goalkeeper. 'When I looked up at the scoreboard and saw there were twenty minutes left, I couldn't believe it,' he said.

'More in your line to keep an eye on the game,' I said. Black humour. What else could we do?

We headed down to Sandymount in a taxi for a drink and walked into a pub around ten in the morning. The barman looked up at us and said, 'Well, lads, were ye at the game yesterday?'

The mood on the train down was dire. We'd been kitted out so we were in new trousers and shirts. Half the lads were still steamed up after the night before, but we were about as low as we could get.

Then we got to Waterford and there was a crowd there waiting for us. That made it worse, them waiting in the rain for us after a performance like that. Little kids with the rain streaming down their faces, singing that Journey song, 'Don't Stop Believing'. To see them stand along the quay in the rain for us . . . we felt we'd let ourselves down and that we'd let them down.

If we could have turned the clock back, we'd have played better, but you can't. That's why you have to give it everything when you have the chance.

We were given a civic reception and then we headed to the Old Stand for a drink. Later on we went to the Granville Hotel. Liam Cusack, the owner, put us up on the Monday night after the final. It was a nice gesture, given where we were. We appreciated it.

The following day, I headed back to Dungarvan and had a couple in Paddy Foley's.

When things settled down, we became more conscious of the criticism – 'Ye got rid of Justin, it serves ye right, ye had it coming,' that kind of thing. Funny, I don't remember any of those experts being in Fraher Field or Walsh Park for the training sessions when the non-starters were feeling ignored. Or when Bryan Phelan was taking twenty penalties in a row. Maybe they're psychic.

Let's not beat around the bush, though. Kilkenny are the best, the top dogs. My only question is whether or not they enjoy winning. They're so used to it, you can hardly tell whether or not they get a kick out of it. The expressions on their faces after beating us wouldn't give anything away: it's just another ordinary day for them.

We've beaten Kilkenny in one or two league games over the last few years and they weren't too happy about it, but they always come back in the championship and they get it right.

To me, it all definitely comes from Brian Cody, that attitude of getting it right or getting out of the way, but they have the advantage of the players to put that attitude into practice.

It's all very well having the approach that if you don't produce the goods then you won't play when there's someone else on the panel there to replace you, but in Kilkenny that's true: there always is someone else. They have a conveyor-belt of young fellas coming through, and there are no distractions. They don't do anything else. There's no soccer, no Gaelic, no rugby. That's a help, but it's only a help to kick things off.

I have total admiration for Cody, the way he's kept his team fresh and hungry. I look at Cody's players and there aren't too many weak links there. Take the defence. Noel Hickey is one tough cookie at full-back, though I wouldn't fear marking him.

The only Kilkenny player I never fancied marking is JJ Delaney: over the years I haven't won too much ball off him, and there have been days when I couldn't get a stroke of the ball off him. It doesn't get any easier when you look at the other backs, but those are two of the best defenders around.

They say the Kilkenny defence get away with murder, but I don't necessarily blame inter-county referees for letting things go. (Maybe it's because of the style of refereeing in Waterford – they don't let things go.) Kilkenny *do* get away with things, but that's the way they've been doing it all their life and they're fantastic at it.

They're sound men when you meet them off the field but they're the best of the best at handing out hammerings in All-Ireland semi-finals and finals, and you have to match their intensity, meet fire with fire. We didn't do it in 2008 – or in 1998 either, when people said they had a poor team.

In 2009 they beat us in the All-Ireland semi-final and we didn't believe we could beat them that day, though we had one or two chances to kill them.

I wouldn't know many of them well but I went to Dave Bennett's stag night in 2010 down in Kilkenny, and we met up with JJ on the night out; we just bumped into him. He was grand, sound as ever, but a few of his mates were smart enough with the comments so we didn't hang around; it was nothing to do with JJ, just the usual thing with the hangers-on.

A real regret is that I didn't make it to the funeral of James McGarry's wife. She had died in a car crash shortly before the 2008 final. When a tragedy like that happens, it underlines the fact that there's a lot more to life than hurling. After Kilkenny won the final, they passed the cup to James and his son. Seeing them lift the cup was a moving sight I'll never forget.

21

We had a terrible holiday after the All-Ireland final – a week in New York. The players weren't too happy with it, but then we had to head back training. The lads weren't in great form for it. That's hardly a surprise – it was always going to be hard to face back into the grind of pre-season training, the hard physical slog, after an All-Ireland final defeat like that.

I wasn't too downhearted for a very simple reason: I felt I couldn't have had a worse year than 2008, so there wasn't much pressure on me to produce miracles. That doesn't mean I was taking it easy – you could ask any of the players, or management, and they'd have to tell you I put in as much effort as any other player. But mentally I felt under less pressure.

I said I'd give it a lash for 2009.

I didn't think of packing it in, but a few of the lads went – Flynn, Dave Bennett, Tom Feeney. You could say that they retired, but I felt they saw the writing on the wall. They hadn't had much game time and that wasn't going to change. It was difficult to see mates that I'd togged out with for ten years just going.

Flynn was a loss. He told me he couldn't stay on with the manager, and that was that. I thought there was definitely another year in him if he put in the effort.

Bennett had been a slow starter, but when he got going he made a huge contribution. He was getting a few injuries, though, and maybe he had had enough.

Tom Feeney was a huge loss too. Compared to top forwards like the other two you mightn't think so, but the work he had done was immense to get where he was, and he would have been an asset to us in 2009.

The training in 2009 was a lot more physical. We'd only had Davy as manager for three months the previous year, and now we had him for the whole season.

We did huge amounts of running, particularly down in Carrick-on-Suir, which I'll always associate with those 2009 sessions for as long as I live. If the lads were playing a game, anyone who didn't play was going around the field – jog, sprint, jog, from one side of the pitch to the other, over and over again.

Now, back from New York, I was struggling with the training, but I stuck with it and got fitter and fitter. It's always tough going back training after taking it easy for a couple of months but if you go off the beer for the few weeks you'll get on top of it, and we did.

But it was savage. There's a place near Kill, a training circuit for horses, and we trained there. Now, I'd thought the sand dunes down in Tramore were bad, and they were bad, but this was diabolical. That was probably great for the young fellas, but Davy made the older lads do it as well, and they got no break in training. I could see the difference in Tony Browne, who didn't come back until March 2009, but he had a great season. He's always training, a natural athlete – as Eoin Kelly says, he's ripped all year round!

A few of us older lads could have done without that slog, and in fairness, Davy seemed to realize this and gave us a different programme in 2010.

There was a lot made of Davy's success with Limerick Institute of Technology in the Fitzgibbon Cup, and college teams are probably good for a manager to learn the ropes, but it's not the same as an inter-county team; it's apples and oranges. Students can take a day off classes to go to the swimming-pool for recovery; you can't do that if you're doing a day's work.

Few people would be aware of the number of days off an inter-county player would need to recover from championship games during the year. A big game takes it out of you. There's huge tension and pressure for days beforehand, then you play and there's a release of tension afterwards. It's almost physical.

I couldn't sleep after the 2004 Munster hurling final. Nothing to do with drink, just the buzz from the day and the game, the entire event. I drank as much as I could that night but I was stone-cold sober going to bed, and I got out of bed at half six to go into the glass factory for work. There was no work done that morning by anyone: they made a huge deal over me. But I couldn't rest, couldn't get any sleep – I took a half-day off that day and the following day.

Anyone who's been through a huge event, like having a child, knows what it's like – you're on such a high you can't sit still and there's no point in trying to rest. (Obviously that's from the father's perspective, as the mother has her hands full . . .) After a championship game it's the same: it's such a big event you have to cut loose. Leave the drink aside: you've got to recover for a day or two.

I thought Davy would have taken all of that on board, but I felt his attitude was strange in 2009. One night in the dressing room before a game, he said, 'I got rid of two whingers we had last year, and anyone who's going to whinge, there's the door.'

Now, I thought he was talking about Flynn and Bennett, two lads who had given thirty years to Waterford between them, and here was a man who had been managing the team for about four months. I looked over at one of the other players and he just shook his head. I'd say Davy's comment was said more for the benefit of some of the young fellas there than anything else. For effect.

But I was seriously pissed off. Flynn might have annoyed him, but they were training as hard as they could. They had to. We all had to in 2008.

The novelty factor with Davy was well gone. I wasn't happy with what he was doing in training, and though I wouldn't be one to confront managers, I'd had enough of him giving out about All-Stars or Hurlers of the Year. He must have known well from my reaction to his drills that I was annoyed with him.

I didn't get many starts in the league, though I came on against Kilkenny and got 1–1 in the only game they lost that year. But my heart wasn't in it. It couldn't be with the manager.

Come the championship, we had Limerick. And Limerick now had Justin McCarthy as manager.

We weren't surprised when he fell in with Limerick. He's too well regarded as a coach to be twiddling his thumbs, and he was always going to get another offer. Once he went to Limerick we all knew well that we were going to be playing Limerick in the championship.

The night they made the draw I watched it on television and I said out loud, 'No doubt about it, we're going to get Limerick.' And Jimmy O'Gorman stuck his hand in the bowl and drew them out. (Jimmy's a legend of a man and we often travelled to games in the same car; to show the calibre of the man, he wrote me a lovely letter when I retired.)

I thought for definite Justin would improve them as a team – they'd been in an All-Ireland final in 2007 – but later in the year they all resigned off the panel, so I suppose they weren't happy with his approach then.

The media made a massive thing out of the fact that we were playing Justin's team, and it nearly worked out perfectly for them: Limerick could have beaten us on the first day we played them.

I came on in the second half. It was a wet day and the final score 1–8 to eleven points tells you everything you need to know.

There wasn't any contact between us and Justin after the match. He didn't come into the dressing room afterwards, which wasn't a surprise.

Two weeks previous to the drawn game, my understanding

was that if I played well in a challenge game against Dublin Davy would start me against Limerick. I scored 1–3 and Davy said afterwards to me, 'You're flying.' But he started Gary Hurney in the second game ahead of me. Gary's a lovely fella but he's a footballer. He wouldn't get the goals I'd get. On top of that, Eoin Kelly was able to tell me the team before it was announced, and I knew I wasn't playing. I called Davy aside and we argued about it. Passionately.

Then, at a training session, I felt he went and made a show of me in front of the entire team – 'No whingers here,' he was saying. 'Any whingers can clear out the gate.'

When he said that, I was looking down at him and thinking, *Will I hit him or just walk out?* In the end I said to myself that I'd stuck it out with Gerald, I'd stuck it out with Justin, and I'd stick it out with Davy too. We had a love–hate relationship.

I suspected that a lot of his attitude in 2009 came from an interview in the papers towards the end of 2008, when Flynn and Bennett were talking about the approach Davy had adopted in the All-Ireland final. He must have been unhappy with that but obviously the two boys were gone from the squad, and his attitude was clear to the rest of us at training – he talked about 'whingers', and getting rid of lads.

We went on to beat Limerick in the replay, then played Tipperary in the Munster final, and there was some change in them from the previous year. Noel McGrath had come in, a fine player, and Padraic Maher, a massive player in the back – you could put him anywhere in the defence and I'd put him centre-back if I were his manager, but I wonder if Conor O'Mahony can play anywhere else apart from number six. No doubt about it, at twenty years of age, Maher's the best young defender around. In the 2009 All-Ireland final he horsed everyone who came near him. Awesome.

The preparations went well, but we didn't do ourselves any favours that day. For one thing, we were getting ourselves right when we heard roaring and shouting outside in the corridor, and someone burst in to tell us that the Waterford minors had won their Munster final. While we were delighted for them, obviously, it was a distraction. You time your countdown to going out on the field for a big game, so that meant we had to readjust and refocus.

The game itself had a very simple bottom line. We conceded four goals; for the fourth, Declan Prendergast slipped up, dropping the ball in front of our goal, and Lar Corbett buried it. We only lost by four points.

I had a decent chance myself of a goal. It was a ball that broke near the Tipperary goal, and I hit it wide; it really irritated me that I didn't at least make Brendan Cummins work to save it. The ball just dribbled wide, and it flashed into my mind: *If that was you a year or two ago, that would have been a goal.*

I knew there was a problem because I thought about hitting it for a split-second. You should never think of it: you should strike the ball on instinct.

It was a heart-breaker because we believed we could beat them, but you can't concede four goals and expect to win any game. Eoin got a goal early on and that was the plan –

to go for goals. No big change there – we know we have to go for goals because over the years we've conceded a good few at the other end. Having said that, the tactics we were using, we never looked like scoring a goal in any game.

Tipp were very good, a young team. They're on the way up – you can see it.

22

In 2009 I felt frustrated after losing the Munster final. It was a disappointing year, but it wasn't as bad as 2003, when we were five points up with ten minutes left against Cork. Who wouldn't be?

But for me it went deeper. Usually I'd go for a few jars after the Munster final – win, lose or draw – but instead I went to Chunky, Peter Kirwan, the physiotherapist, for some rehab, and I made up my mind on the way home: I was packing it in.

I pulled the car into the side of the road on the way back from Chunky's in Kill. There were tears in my eyes, sitting in the car after making the decision. I rang my father and he said, 'I understand.' It was emotional enough for him too. He had great days out following us, and I'm proud of that. But, as I said to him, he had my brother Maurice coming through.

I discussed it with Colette, and she said it was my decision; she wouldn't make a big deal of it.

I rang Eoin, and told him. I spoke to my uncle, and that was nearly as emotional as talking to my father. 'You don't owe anybody anything,' he said to me. 'You've given us great days out – but don't rush your decision.'

It's a real milestone when you finally hang it up. It means something more than just opting out of a team. I suppose it means I'm not a young man any more. I was saying to myself that I was too old for it . . .

Davy Fitzgerald had got wind of my decision to retire, because he rang me then. 'Don't rush into anything,' he said. 'Come back training and see how you go.'

I can be negative enough about him but I'd give him credit for that – he was good to me at that time. I thought about it. It was the middle of the season, and after making the kind of effort we all need to make to get ourselves right for the year, I'd be foolish to throw it away in the middle of the summer.

As I'd said to my father, Maurice had joined the senior team. It wasn't a surprise to me – he had always stood out at underage level because of his ability to hit frees, all the way up. I hadn't seen the years going by, but all of a sudden he was eighteen, he was getting more scores than me . . . There's thirteen years between us, but I turned around and there he was on the county senior team.

He found the training hard, no doubt about that. He was sent for medical tests, as all new players are, to make sure he could take it, and once he cleared those he was put through the mill. But when you're young, you can take it. You're knackered after training but you can go again the following evening. And Maurice is naturally fit. On the runs, he'd lap me if he got half a chance, which brought me back to 1996, and the days I'd be lapping the likes of Damien Byrne. Now I'm the older lad and Maurice is lapping me. The wheel always turns, I suppose, and at this stage I'd have to cheat a bit in the sprints not to be embarrassed totally.

Anyway, you have to use the head when it comes to training. I'd never break my back early on in the season: I'd have nothing left for the championship if I did. I'm better off being at the back of the pack doing the laps at the start of the year, so when I start moving towards the front of the bunch as the weeks go by I can point to my progress. That was always my master plan.

I encourage Maurice, and tell him to enjoy it, but I don't tell him what to do. He knows well himself what to do. I'd often argue with him – 'Why didn't you leave it into me?' that kind of thing – but he'll argue his point back. He's getting stronger and stronger; he's where he should be for twenty years of age.

I went back. There was too much work done to turn my back then. The year wasn't going great but I said I'd stick with it.

We played Galway in the qualifiers, and after they'd beaten Cork well in the previous game, I've no doubt they underestimated us. They were on top of us, too, but they couldn't put us away. I didn't start the game, and it was one day I was raring to go. After the warm-up I never felt better. I felt strong and ready; I never felt more positive that I'd be all right, that I was able for the day.

I genuinely felt with half an hour to go that I'd change the game if I was put on, but Davy brought on a couple of other lads – Shane Walsh and Maurice – and I said nothing. With a few minutes to go we were in dire straits, and Davy told me to warm up. Ken McGrath was injured and sitting on the bench, and he said to me, 'Go in there and do the business for us, Dan.'

Six minutes to go and Davy called me out, but I wasn't listening when he was giving me his instructions. We were in deep shit, four points down, and all I was thinking was, *I'm going to shove this up his hole now. I'll show him*.

I went in on Eugene McEntee, who was full-back. Shane Kavanagh had broken his hand the previous day against Cork and McEntee was making his debut. I got the first ball that came in and shaved the post with the shot; if anything I hit it too well, and it just went the wrong side of the post.

They went down the field and attacked, and Ger Farragher tried to be extra sure of his pass, but Aidan Kearney came across the field, won it for us, and just launched it downfield – no look up, thanks, Aidan. It landed between me and McEntee.

I won that as well, and I glanced up and saw Ollie Canning for Galway was too far off Shane Walsh; he had come in to back up McEntee, but when I caught the ball he was in no man's land, not close enough to me and too far from Shane.

That's where a bit of common sense and experience come into it: if you're getting tackled by two or three players, then there has to be someone free beyond them that you can get the ball to, if you keep your head. And that was what happened. I popped it over Canning's head for Shane Walsh – that's one thing the lads would have to admit, I'd never hog the ball – and he buried it. I was delighted for Shane Walsh, who had put a lot of effort in over the years, as well as Shane Casey, who played well that day.

They pucked the ball out and we won it, and when it landed in the full-forward line, I won it, and got a free. A debatable enough one, but we took it.

We had the upper hand. You know it in a game – you can almost smell it; you can see it in the crowd. The Waterford supporters knew Galway were gone. I knew we were going to win it. We had the spark and they were rocked back.

Declan Prendergast burst out of defence in the last minute, carried the ball upfield and popped it to Mullane. He put over the winner.

At the final whistle everybody came over to me, clapping me on the back. For the six minutes I got, I was delighted. Afterwards, Davy said to me, 'I knew you'd do it. I had faith in you.'

I was thinking, *You did, yeah, you had no more faith in me now, after giving me just six minutes of play*.

I thought he was trying to finish me.

RTÉ called me out for an interview. It had been a couple of years since I was asked, so that brought it home to me. I'd been out of the limelight.

Of course, I had a pink T-shirt on me – waiting to head out on the lash – and they cut me to pieces over it. Back in the dressing room, though, Gerry Fitzpatrick said, 'Lads, if you're going to go on the beer it's a waste of time,' and we abided by that, which meant my pink T-shirt got no air time. We had great time for Gerry.

I was offered money for an interview by a journalist and I did the right thing: I asked Davy about it. He said no, because he didn't like the journalist. I said he'd offered me money, and Davy said he'd prefer I didn't do it because of something that that journalist had written, something Davy didn't like.

So there was a fair few bob gone west, thanks to the man who was writing for the *Star*. He was the manager and it was his right to say he didn't want me to do the interview. But it annoyed me – a lot.

We had Kilkenny in the semi-final in 2009 and, no, the fairy-tale ending didn't come through. They beat us by only five points, which was a fair turnaround after the previous year's horror show, but it was still a loss in an All-Ireland semi-final.

On the bus out of Croke Park I had a think about packing it in. I was thirty-two and didn't look to have a future on the team as a starting player, and the training was getting harder and harder. I knew, even as the bus was pulling out, that experts and supporters were probably counting out on their fingers how many of us would be back the following year – or which of us wouldn't, which would make it easier for them.

With the evidence they had to go on, I was probably top of their list of retirements. Were they right? I looked up and down the aisle of the bus at the lads and thought of what 2010 might hold. For the team. For me.

People ask how we carry on playing in Waterford without winning an All-Ireland, after all the disappointments. How can we keep facing the training, the nights stuck in at home, the abuse when we don't win anything? The abuse even when we win something.

If you were part of the team and you'd travelled the road with us, you'd understand.

A team is much more than a group of lads who get together on a Sunday afternoon to play a match. It has to be. To tell the other fellas who tog on with you that you're willing to go the extra mile for them, you have to mean it. That takes time. It takes time to build a team but it's worth the effort. You don't know it until you're part of one, and then you never forget it.

A fair example is what happened to me back in 1999, when Colette had Chloe. The lads were delighted for me, because I was one of the first players on the team to have a baby. But it went further than a few fellas saying congratulations in the dressing room and shaking my hand. They were practical. Ken and Eoin were only young lads then – teenagers – but when Colette and Chloe were still in Ardkeen hospital, they insisted that I stay over in their houses in Waterford city rather than hitting the road back down to Dungarvan late at night.

Flynner was very good too. He can come across as odd, but that time he called down to the hospital one evening and brought me back up to his place for dinner. You don't coach fellas into behaving like that, or tell them to act that way. They either know to do that kind of thing, to offer that kind of help, or they don't. They did, and I've never forgotten them for it.

It's not always serious death-or-glory stuff. If it was, we wouldn't be long getting tired of it.

Myself and Ken had some shenanigans on one team holiday, when we ended up going to Morocco – the worst team holiday ever. The first night we were there, Ken, Kelly and myself went out to get our bearings and try to pick up the local lingo – i.e. go on the batter. We were trying to find some place decent for the night but we had a fair struggle. On the way back to the hotel, we were messing and I ended up breaking a huge shop window.

Christ. I was thinking *Midnight Express* if the cops collared us, so I legged it back to the hotel to get the wallet, just to cover the expense of replacing the window. Bigger fool that I was, I left it down on the wall behind me at one stage and when I turned around it was gone.

Great stuff, Dan. First night on the holiday and all my cash whipped.

The lads dipped into their own pockets and sorted me out. Ken was in charge of that: he made sure everybody gave me what they could. Outstanding stuff. Of course, I put a fair hole in the dig-out the lads gave me. I was on holiday: what else was I going to do?

The last night in Morocco, Ken and myself went out again. We didn't have much money left at that stage but at least I didn't break any shop windows this time. We went hard at it and ended up on the whiskey. The cash ran dry before our appetites, and nothing would do us only to stay drinking.

The solution? I had a pair of white Adidas runners on me and we sold them to a lad in the bar for a few more drops of whiskey.

Then there was one night we were on holiday in New York in 2007 and, as usual, one of the nights we were let out for a few drinks. One of the lads – who'll have to remain nameless – happened to be rooming near to Justin that week, and when some of us rolled back after the night on the lash he flicked on the porn channel.

Cue Justin coming out of his room and hammering on our man's door. Door opens and the Riot Act gets read. Door closes. Justin goes back to his room. The porn soundtrack gets turned up even louder.

As the bus rolled through Dublin following our defeat to Kilkenny, there were still people in white and blue on the streets. They cheered us and clapped. They appreciate what we're doing.

And we appreciate them. We don't know how lucky we are to be able to play hurling. I give Davy huge credit for bringing kids who are sick or disabled along to training to meet us all, and he often reminds us, 'Don't ever forget how lucky ye are.'

He's right. I see kids in wheelchairs coming in to watch us training and I realize they'll never enjoy a game of hurling, or it sinks in how much care and attention their family gives them. You wouldn't be long remembering how lucky you are then.

I thank God every day that Chloe is happy and healthy, so if the community in Waterford is ever looking for our support – for cancer services in the south-east or anything like that – I'm more than happy to help out.

I'm part of that community, after all. I might be playing for the county in front of a big crowd in Thurles or Croke Park, there's huge coverage in the media, people say it's life-or-death and take it very seriously . . . But when I come home from those games I'm part of the community, just as I'm part of the community when I'm playing for Waterford.

I represent people but I'm one of them as well. Inter-county players don't live in some vast mansion miles from anywhere, like a Premiership player: they're doing their shopping in the supermarket with everybody else; they're going to mass and parent–teacher meetings like everybody else.

Just because I wear a jersey on the occasional Sunday doesn't mean I'm better than anybody else, and I'd certainly hope people would never be able to accuse me of being big-headed. I've won a lot of awards and medals, but if anyone said I was unrecognizable from the youngster who was almost too shy to speak at that first training session in 1996, I'd be hugely disappointed. In myself.

I sat back on the bus and said I'd give it one more year.

17 July 2010: Semple Stadium, Munster Final replay

It's almost twelve months later. We've beaten Clare in the semi-final of the Munster Championship, and have drawn against Cork in a tight match, though I haven't got much game time. We're out for the replay the following Saturday night.

A Munster hurling final on a Saturday night has got to be the craziest decision of all time, and nobody's happy with it. The GAA says it's a matter of promotion with the Ulster and Connacht football finals on the Sunday, but there are more people in Thurles at seven p.m., late as it is, than there are at the Connacht final.

Ding-dong battle. Eoin misses a couple of frees towards the end of normal time, but when we go into the dressing room before extra time the mood is still good.

Brian O'Halloran has been sent on, as I knew he would be. At training the previous Tuesday Davy was talking to the forwards and said, 'You listen to this too, Brian,' and I guessed he'd be brought in. He's fast and he does well, scoring a point, but I can't pretend . . . I wish I was out there myself.

I'm out beyond the dressing room when Ken comes over. 'We're surely worth five minutes out there,' he says.

'We are, Mac, we'll get our chance,' I say.

Mullane then says he's got cramp.

'Are you okay to play or will I start someone instead of you?' says Davy.

'Start someone,' he says. 'I can't play with this.'

'Dan,' says Davy, 'you're going in at centre-forward.'

Mullane's honest. Another player might have continued, but not him.

Out on the field I bless myself, and Tom Kenny's at centre-back. The usual welcome. No worries there.

Brick wins the clash, pops the ball to me and I give it to Kevin Moran. Point.

Then . . .

We attack and the ball comes out to me from Eoin McGrath. I think I might get caught by a covering defender, and I expect a Cork player to tackle me straight away, but there's nothing. Nobody near me. I'm a good twenty yards out but I feel confident. I've a decent record against Cork when it comes to scoring goals.

It crosses my mind for a split-second about carrying it in a bit, but I look up to see where Dónal Óg Cusack is in the goal.

He steps out from the line, just one or two steps – he's expecting me to carry it in and he's getting himself ready. He shimmies a little bit to his right, and that opens up the goal a little on his left-hand side.

He doesn't move by much, but I figure I may catch him if I go early, so I let fly. I connect well with the ball but it doesn't shoot off the wet grass like I hope – it's as if it gets caught a little in it, if anything. Dónal Óg gets his hurley to it all right but it carries on and rolls into the corner of the net. Goal.

I don't think it was the end of the game – this is Cork–Waterford, it's never over until the final whistle – but I know it's a huge blow for them.

I jog back out to centre-forward. It's not a time for big celebrations. Not during the game, anyway.

At the final whistle my goal separates the two teams, and the entire Waterford bench sprints towards me. Maurice is the first man to me; we've won a Munster final together, the two Shanahan brothers.

A couple of evenings later Mullane will tell me it's the only time I ran all night, getting away from my team-mates at the final whistle.

Not a bad shot. We won. I'll take that.

Epilogue

15 August 2010: Croke Park, All Ireland Semi-final

The dressing room is silent. Davy and Stephen Molumphy have said their few words, thanking us for our efforts, but it's no consolation. We never got going against Tipperary at all, and the game was over as a contest long before the end. I'm disappointed I didn't get on earlier; as I was fixing my helmet straps to come on in the second half Eoin Kelly got Tipp's second goal to kill the game.

In my opinion this was a game that Waterford lost – we were too caught up in the tactics we were given. I was disappointed that I hadn't had more game time as I was going well in training. A few weeks later I happened to read in a newspaper that the players themselves did not stick to their tactics. People might say that the tactics worked in other games, but for big games against big teams we should have gone man for man. We played into Tipp's hands the way we played that day. The past six or seven years Waterford played attractive hurling and were enjoyable to watch but that has gone, the way we are playing now. God be with the days Waterford would get three or four goals in a game – not any more. I know the game has changed – work rate, etc – but I don't think Waterford hurling should have changed. That's not just my opinion.

The Tipp manager, Liam Sheedy, was honest and generous when he came in to sympathize. He paid tribute to us and what we've done for hurling. I have plenty of time for Sheedy. He speaks from the heart.

Now I'm about to do the same. Mark O'Brien is on one side of me in the dressing room, a lad trying to get established on the team, and Ken is on the other side: one of the all-time greats. One lad's done it all and the other is trying to make his name; the two sides of the same coin.

I stand up and clear my throat.

'Lads, I just want to say something.

'This is my last day with ye, my last day in the dressing room. I want to say how much I've enjoyed it, how much I've appreciated everything – the good times and the bad times – and how much respect I have for my team-mates.

'I know this isn't the end for the team, but it's the end for me with Waterford. I'd like to think I've made some good friends here over the years and I'd also like to think I haven't lost any.

'Thank you all very much.'

The lads clap. Some of them come over and shake hands. Tony's shaking his head. I'm not ashamed to say I have tears in my eyes.

I take a long look around before we head out of the dressing-room door. I won't be back here, so I want to take it in, but all I can see are the lads I've sweated and bled with for all these years. That's the memory I take out of the place.

We walk out of Croke Park, out onto Jones's Road. There are a few loyal souls in white and blue still there, and they come up and shake hands with us as the sun sets.

And I ask myself the same question that was in my head seven months ago.

Where did the time go?

Dan Shanahan – Record for Waterford

Date	Competition	Venue	Opponent	Score	Result
24 May 1998	Munster Quarter-Final	Austin Stack Park, Tralee	Kerry	0–6	0–20 : 1–09
7 Jun 1998	Munster Semi-Final	Páirc Uí Chaoimh, Cork	Tipperary	0–2	0–21 : 2–12
12 Jul 1998	Munster Final	Semple Stadium, Thurles	Clare	0–3	3–10 : 1–16
19 Jul 1998	Munster Final Replay	Semple Stadium, Thurles	Clare	0–0	0–10 : 2–16
26 Jul 1998	All-Ireland Quarter-Final	Croke Park, Dublin	Galway	0–1	1–20 : 1–10
16 Aug 1998	All-Ireland Semi-Final	Croke Park, Dublin	Kilkenny	0–2	1–10 : 1–11
30 May 1999	Munster Quarter-Final	Semple Stadium, Thurles	Limerick	0–1	1–16 : 1–15
14 Jun 1999	Munster Semi-Final	Semple Stadium, Thurles	Cork	0–3	1–15 : 0–24
28 May 2000	Munster Quarter-Final	Páirc Uí Chaoimh, Cork	Tipperary	0–1	0–14 : 0–17
10 Jun 2001	Munster Semi-Final	Páirc Uí Chaoimh, Cork	Limerick	0–1	2–14 : 4–11
26 May 2002	Munster Semi-Final	Semple Stadium, Thurles	Cork	0–0	1–16 : 1–15
30 Jun 2002	Munster Final	Páirc Uí Chaoimh, Thurles	Tipperary	0–0	2–23 : 3–12
11 Aug 2002	All-Ireland Semi-Final	Croke Park, Dublin	Clare	0–0	1–13 : 1–16
11 May 2003	Munster Quarter-Final	Walsh Park, Waterford	Kerry	0–1	2–26 : 1–12
1 Jun 2003	Munster Semi-Final	Semple Stadium, Thurles	Limerick	0–0	4–13 : 4–13
8 Jun 2003	Munster Semi-Final Replay	Semple Stadium, Thurles	Limerick	0–1	1–12 : 0–13
20 Jul 2003	3rd Round Qualifier	Nolan Park, Kilkenny	Wexford	0–1	0–18 : 1–20
16 May 2004	Munster Quarter-Final	Semple Stadium, Thurles	Clare	3–1	3–21 : 1–8
6 Jun 2004	Munster Semi-Final	Páirc Uí Chaoimh, Cork	Tipperary	2–0	4–10 : 3–12
27 Jun 2004	Munster Final	Semple Stadium, Thurles	Cork	1–3	3–16 : 1–21
8 Aug 2004	All-Ireland Semi-Final	Croke Park, Dublin	Kilkenny	0–0	0–18 : 3–12
22 May 2005	Munster Semi-Final	Semple Stadium, Thurles	Cork	1–0	2–15 : 2–17
18 Jun 2005	Group Stage. Qualifier	Dr Cullen Park, Carlow	Offaly	0–0	1–26 : 1–15
2 Jul 2005	Group Stage Qualifier	Walsh Park, Waterford	Dublin	0–0	4–17 : 1–3

9 Jul 2005	Group Stage Qualifier	Cusack Park, Ennis	Clare	0–3	0–21 : 4–14
24 Jul 2005	All-Ireland Quarter-Final	Croke Park, Dublin	Cork	1–0	1–13 : 1–18
4 Jun 2006	Munster Semi-Final	Páirc Uí Chaoimh, Cork	Tipperary	1–0	1–12 : 3–14
18 Jun 2006	Group Stage Qualifier	Cusack Park, Mullingar	Westmeath	1–2	3–22 : 1–14
2 Jul 2006	Group Stage Qualifier	Walsh Park, Waterford	Galway	0–2	1–25 : 2–20
8 Jul 2006	Group Stage Qualifier	O'Moore Park, Portlaoise	Laois	0–0	2–17 : 1–13
23 Jul 2006	All-Ireland Quarter-Final	Croke Park, Dublin	Tipperary	1–5	1–22 : 3–13
6 Aug 2006	All-Ireland Semi-Final	Croke Park, Dublin	Cork	0–1	1–15 : 1–16
17 Jun 2007	Munster Semi-Final	Semple Stadium, Thurles	Cork	2–1	5–15 : 3–18
8 Jul 2007	Munster Final	Semple Stadium, Thurles	Limerick	3–3	3–17 : 1–14
29 Jul 2007	All-Ireland Quarter-Final	Croke Park, Dublin	Cork	1–3	3–16 : 3–16
5 Aug 2007	All-Ireland Quarter-Final Replay	Croke Park, Dublin	Cork	2–1	2–17 : 0–20
12 Aug 2007	All-Ireland Semi-Final	Croke Park, Dublin	Limerick	0–4	2–15 : 5–11
1 Jun 2008	Munster Quarter-Final	Gaelic Grounds, Limerick	Clare	0–0	0–23 : 2–26
5 Jul 2008	2nd Round Qualifier	Walsh Park, Waterford	Antrim	0–4	6–18 : 0–15
19 Jul 2008	4th Round Qualifier	Semple Stadium, Thurles	Offaly	0–0	2–18 : 0–18
27 Jul 2008	All-Ireland Quarter-Final	Semple Stadium, Thurles	Wexford	1–1	2–19 : 3–15
17 Aug 2008	All-Ireland Semi-Final	Croke Park, Dublin	Tipperary	0–0	1–20 : 1–18
7 Sep 2008	All-Ireland Final	Croke Park, Dublin	Kilkenny	0–0	1–13 : 3–30
14 Jun 2009	Munster Semi-Final	Semple Stadium, Thurles	Limerick	0–0	0–11 : 1–08
20 Jun 2009	Munster Semi-Final Replay	Semple Stadium, Thurles	Limerick	0–0	0–25 : 0–17
12 Jul 2009	Munster Final	Semple Stadium, Thurles	Tipperary	0–1	2–16 : 4–14
26 Jul 2009	All-Ireland Quarter-Final	Semple Stadium, Thurles	Galway	0–0	1–16 : 0–18
9 Aug 2009	All-Ireland Semi-Final	Croke Park, Dublin	Kilkenny	0–1	3–15 : 2–23
7 Jun 2010	Munster Semi-Final	Semple Stadium, Thurles	Clare	0–0	0–22 : 1–15
11 Jul 2010	Munster Final	Semple Stadium, Thurles	Cork	0–0	2–15 : 2–15
17 Jul 2010	Munster Final Replay	Semple Stadium, Thurles	Cork	1–0	1–16 : 1–13
15 Aug 2010	All-Ireland Semi-Final	Croke Park, Dublin	Tipperary	0–0	1–18 : 3–19

Picture Acknowledgements

Unless otherwise credited, all the photos have been kindly supplied by the author. The publishers have made every effort to contact copyright holders where known. Copyright holders who have not been credited are invited to get in touch.

Credits run clockwise from top left.

Section one

Pages 2/3: 1998 All-Ireland semi-final v. Kilkenny: courtesy *Irish Examiner*; DS and Davy Fitzgerald: © Inpho/Patrick Bolger; Munster semi-final, 2004: Brendan Moran/Sportsfile; Munster final replay, 1998: courtesy *Irish Examiner*.

Pages 4/5: Munster final, 2004: © Inpho/Patrick Bolger; DS and Diarmuid O'Sullivan: © Inpho/Morgan Treacy; DS and Seán Óg Ó hAilpín: courtesy *Irish Examiner*.

Pages 6/7: DS and Justin McCarthy: David Maher/Sportsfile; All-Ireland quarter-final, 2007, DS scoring: David Maher/Sportsfile; DS and Gerald McCarthy: David Maher/Sportsfile; All-Ireland quarter-final: © Inpho/Billy Strickland.

Page 8: DS and Brian O'Driscoll: Brendan Moran/Sportsfile; DS with Bertie Ahern and Nicky Brennan: Ray McManus/Sportsfile.

Section two

Pages 2/3, from top right: DS kissing the crest: courtesy *Irish Examiner*; DS's tattoo: courtesy *Irish Examiner*; DS and Chloe: Stephen McCarthy/Sportsfile.

Pages 4/5: DS and Justin McCarthy: Brendan Moran/Sportsfile; DS and Davy Fitzgerald: Stephen McCarthy/Sportsfile; DS and Brendan Cummins: Stephen McCarthy/Sportsfile; DS and Eoin Kelly: Matt Browne/Sportsfile; DS and John Mullane: © Inpho/Cathal Noonan.

Pages 6/7: DS, Noel Hickey and JJ Delaney: © Inpho/James Crombie; Munster final replay, 2010: Sportsfile/Ray McManus; celebrating goal: Brendan Moran/Sportsfile.

Page 8: moment of victory, Munster final: © Inpho/Cathal Noonan.

Index